CHRISTIAN FOUNDATIONS

A series edited by

PHILIP E. HUGHES

8

CHRIST'S AMBASSADORS

Raymond E. Morton
1969

These books appear under the auspices of the Evangelical Fellowship in the Anglican Communion, which unites evangelical Anglican fellowships and individuals in many parts of the world

The Reverend Frank Colquhoun, M.A. (Durham), Canon Residentiary of Southwark Cathedral and Examining Chaplain to the Bishop of Southwark, has also written:

Harringay Story

Your Child's Baptism
  (Christian Commitment Series)

The Gospels

The Catechism and The Order of Confirmation
  (Prayer Book Commentaries)

Total Christianity

He was formerly Editor of:

The Churchman

He was Editor of the symposium:

The Living Church in The Parish

CHRISTIAN FOUNDATIONS

CHRIST'S AMBASSADORS

THE PRIORITY OF PREACHING

by

FRANK COLQUHOUN

HODDER AND STOUGHTON

Copyright © 1965 by The Evangelical Fellowship
in the Anglican Communion

First printed 1965

This book is sold subject to the conditions that it shall not by way of trade be lent, re-sold, hired out, or otherwise disposed of without the publisher's consent in any form of binding or cover other than that in which it is published.

Printed in Great Britain for Hodder and Stoughton Limited,
St. Paul's House, Warwick Lane, London, E.C.4,
by Hazell Watson & Viney Ltd, Aylesbury, Bucks

FOREWORD

by HIS GRACE THE MOST REVD. HUGH R. GOUGH, O.B.E., D.D., *Archbishop of Sydney and Primate of Australia, President of the Evangelical Fellowship in the Anglican Communion.*

IN these days Anglicanism has become aware in a new way that it has a world-wide mission, not to preserve itself but to give itself, and if necessary to lose itself, in the service of others. At the 1963 Toronto Congress, the Archbishop of Canterbury admonished Anglicans that 'the church that lives to itself will die by itself', and Bishop Stephen Bayne insisted that the end of Anglican missionary strategy was not that there should be more Anglicans but that the Church of Jesus Christ should be planted in every place. The formation of united regional churches along the lines of the Church of South India will mean the diminishment and perhaps the ultimate disappearance of Anglicanism—except in so far as it may well be representative of a united national church in England.

None can fail to be involved in this process of transition and realignment in the history of the Christian Church, and evangelicals have a full and essential contribution to make. This present series of books in the CHRISTIAN FOUNDATIONS series is one evidence of the earnestness of evangelicals and their determination to give of their best in the cause of Christ's Kingdom. In these books Anglican evangelical scholars address themselves to themes, theological and practical, which are of vital significance for the Christian Church. They do so in a manner which is scriptural, contemporary, and, of course, evangelical. Though directed to the Anglican situation, the outlook is not narrowly limited to Anglicanism. These books have a truly catholic scope, and accordingly they can speak with clarity and also charity to those on either side of Anglicanism, and indeed, to many who at present are outside the fellowship of Christian believers. I commend this CHRISTIAN FOUNDATIONS series cordially and with confidence, and trust that it will be read widely throughout and beyond the Anglican Communion.

HUGH SYDNEY

ACKNOWLEDGEMENTS

The Author wishes to express his thanks for the permission which has been granted to quote from the following works.

Donald Coggan, *Stewards of Grace* (Hodder and Stoughton, Ltd., London).

H. H. Farmer, *The Servant of the Word* (James Nisbet and Co., Ltd., London).

Hastings' *Dictionary of Christ and the Gospels*, Vol. II, article 'Preaching Christ' by James Denney (T. and T. Clark, Edinburgh).

Hamish C. Mackenzie, *Preaching the Eternities* (Saint Andrew Press, Edinburgh).

James S. Stewart, *Heralds of God* (Hodder and Stoughton, Ltd., London).

J.-J. Von Allen, *Preaching and Congregation* (Lutterworth Press, London).

CONTENTS

		Page
	Foreword by the Most Revd. Hugh R. Gough, Primate of Australia	5
1	THE PRIORITY OF PREACHING	11
2	WHAT IS PREACHING?	24
3	PREACHING AND THE BIBLE	40
4	PREACHING AND WORSHIP	59
5	PREACHING TODAY	77

Note: Quotations from the Bible are, in general, from the Revised Standard Version.

CHAPTER ONE

THE PRIORITY OF PREACHING

THE New Testament record of our Lord's Galilean ministry begins with the words, 'Jesus came ... preaching the gospel of God' (Mk. 1:14). The simple statement is pregnant with meaning. It confronts us with a picture which dominates a large area of the Gospels. Jesus stands before us not simply as the mighty miracle-worker or the zealous social reformer but supremely as the bearer of good tidings from God to men.

'God had only one Son,' remarked the Puritan Thomas Goodwin, 'and He made Him a preacher.' No one can deny that Jesus Himself attached priority to His preaching. When He opened His ministry in the synagogue at Nazareth He took as His text the words of Isaiah: 'The Spirit of the Lord is upon me, because He has anointed me to preach good news to the poor ...' (see Lk. 4:18f.). And as He spoke the eyes of all were fixed upon Him, and they were astonished by the words of grace that fell from His lips.

From that memorable occasion onwards, right through His ministry, Jesus put preaching first. We see Him preaching in the synagogue at Capernaum on the sabbath, and preaching in such a way that again the people were amazed, because His word was with authority. We see Him preaching by the shore of the Sea of Galilee, using Peter's fishing boat for His pulpit since 'the people pressed upon Him to hear the word of God'. We see Him going up the mountainside and preaching the most memorable of all His sermons to the crowds that gathered. The comment of the Evangelist, 'the common people heard Him gladly', bears witness to the popularity as well as to the power of His preaching. Even His critics were compelled to admit, 'No man ever spoke like this man!'

True, Jesus was a prophet mighty in deed as well as in word, and His works of compassion were not without their significance. They vindicated and illustrated His teaching. They testified to His divine origin. In a profound sense they were the kingdom of God in action. But it is clear that Jesus Himself attached primary importance to His preaching rather than to His miracles. He refused to be diverted from His main work by the clamour of the crowd for spectacular signs. When, after healing the sick at Capernaum, He was told, 'Every one is searching for you', He said to His disciples, 'Let us go on to the next towns, that I may preach there also; for that is why I came out' (Mk. 1: 35–39). Before Pontius Pilate He declared, 'For this I was born, and for this I have come into the world, to bear witness to the truth' (Jn. 18: 37). And in sending out His disciples on their first mission tour it is noteworthy that He put preaching first, and healing second (Lk. 9: 2).

Christ's last great commission to His Church was to evangelize the world. How was it to be done? By preaching! His apostles were to make disciples of all nations by preaching the good news to all nations (cf. Mt. 28: 18 and Lk. 24: 47). This was the Lord's strategy for His Church in relation to the world. It is still His plan today.

THE EARLY CHURCH

From the very beginning the Church was a preaching Church. The apostles put preaching in the forefront of their programme. Their priorities were clear: 'We will devote ourselves to prayer and to the ministry of the word' (Acts 6:4). The story of Acts impressively illustrates the place of preaching in the beginnings of Christianity. Take, for example, the record of the day of Pentecost, so often called the birthday of the Christian Church. In what way was the Church thus brought to birth? Again the answer is—by preaching! As a result, three thousand were added to the Lord and His people, having been 'born anew, not of perishable seed but of imperishable, through the living and abiding word of God'—that word being 'the good news which was preached' (see I Pet. 1:23–25). Pentecost not only bears witness to the transforming power of the Spirit of God in the life of the Church. It also testifies to the regenerating power of the Word of God when preached to men in the energy of the same Spirit.

Again and again in Acts the picture of the preaching Church is brought before our notice. The apostles quite literally meant it when they declared before their judges, 'We cannot but speak of what we have seen and heard' (4:20). They were imprisoned and beaten and forbidden to preach; but still they could not desist. 'Every day in the temple and at home they did not cease teaching and preaching Jesus Christ' (5.42). Moreover, they refused to get sidetracked from this primary task by the demands of church administration, and said so plainly. 'It is not right that we should give up preaching the word of God to serve tables' (6:2). Others were appointed to do this; but of the seven thus chosen, two at least became notable preachers. Stephen preached with such power that those who disputed with him 'could not withstand the wisdom and the Spirit with which he spoke' (6:10). Shortly after he was to seal his testimony with his blood; but from that dying witness of his sprang, in all likelihood, the conversion of Saul of Tarsus. The other member of the Seven whose preaching is reported is Philip, who proclaimed the Christ in a city of Samaria and also to a solitary traveller in the desert (8:5, 35).

One thing is clear from Acts: persecution could not silence the Church's witness. After the first opposition on the part of the Jerusalem authorities we are told that the Spirit-filled company 'spoke the word of God with boldness' and that 'with great power the apostles gave their testimony to the resurrection of the Lord Jesus' (4:31, 33). Later the pressure became such that the Church was scattered throughout the region; but it was still a preaching Church. 'Those who were scattered went about preaching the word' (8:4). Herod's attack at a later stage still had much the same effect: 'the word of God grew and multiplied' (12:24).

THE APOSTLE PAUL

In the second part of Acts the towering figure of St. Paul dominates the scene. He does so supremely as a missionary preacher. His extensive travels throughout the Roman Empire were not sight-seeing tours but evangelistic journeys, designed to blaze a trail for the Gospel.

Undoubtedly Paul was a man of varied accomplishments and his ministry was many-sided. But first and foremost he was a preacher. 'Christ sent me,' he declared to the

Corinthians, 'not to baptize, but to preach the gospel' (I Cor. 1: 17). In saying that, the apostle was not disparaging the sacrament of baptism but magnifying the office of preaching. Preaching was his business. He had no choice in the matter. 'If I preach the gospel,' he asserted, 'that gives me no ground for boasting. For necessity is laid upon me. Woe to me if I do not preach the gospel!' (I Cor. 9: 16).

Preaching the Gospel was, for Paul, not only an inescapable duty. It was a divine obligation. It was the *raison d'être* of his ministry, the thing he was born to do in the purpose of God. He bears witness to this in his epistle to the Galatians: 'In His good pleasure God, who had set me apart from birth and called me through His grace, chose to reveal His Son to me and through me, in order that I might proclaim Him among the Gentiles' (1: 15, 16, N. E. B.).

He says much the same thing in Ephesians when he explains that he was made a minister of the Gospel in accordance with the gift of God's grace, and adds, 'To me, though I am the very least of all the saints, this grace was given, to preach to the Gentiles the unsearchable riches of Christ' (3: 7, 8). And in sharing his missionary plans with the Romans he says that it is the one ambition of his life to preach Christ's Gospel in those places where His name has never been heard (15: 20).

Paul was deeply sensible of the fact that he had been put in trust with the Gospel. That Gospel he envisaged as the 'deposit' of revealed truth which the Lord had committed to him—and which he in turn must commit to the Lord (see II Tim. 1: 12 mg.). Though Paul delighted to speak of it as 'my Gospel', he knew that in the deepest sense it was not his at all. He had not originated it. Christ had given it to him. Nor was it for him alone. Christ had given it to him that he might give it to others. It was meant for everybody, for the whole world. Therefore the whole world must hear it.

But before Paul could preach the Gospel to others he had first to appropriate it for himself. And that is why he could with perfect accuracy speak of 'my Gospel'. Not only had he received it at first-hand from the Lord: he had bound its glowing message to his heart. Indeed, the Gospel had become part of himself. So thoroughly had he believed it, so deeply had it penetrated his life, that henceforth Paul and the Gospel were inseparable. His whole soul was aflame with the glory of its message. 'I am eager to preach the gospel to you,' he testified to the Romans. 'For I am not ashamed of the gospel: it is the power of God for salvation to every one who has faith' (1:15, 16).

Not to the apostle Paul alone but to Christ's people of every age and in every place belongs the same sacred charge, the same burning mission. The Church as a whole is put in trust with the Gospel. Apart from the Gospel the Church has no existence, and therefore no function. For the Church both lives *by* the Gospel and *for* the Gospel. And the Gospel, by its very nature, compels utterance. It is of such a character that it must be preached. There is, no doubt, such a thing as is piously described as a 'silent witness'; but to speak of a silent church is really sheer nonsense. If a church is silent it is not the Church.

The long centuries of Christian history bear ample witness to the truth that whenever the Church has been most loyal to its commission and to its Lord it has put preaching in the forefront of its programme. The glorious epochs of evangelical awakening and spiritual advance have been those in which the pulpit has been honoured and the Word of God has been sounded out without fear and without compromise. On the other hand, the decline of gospel preaching has consistently been accompanied by the decline of vital Christianity. Whenever the Word of God is dethroned, superstition speedily reigns in its place.

The story of the English Church in the sixteenth century illustrates that only too plainly. The Dark Ages were dark because the Word of God was not preached to men. When with the Reformation the light of God broke through the darkness, the sermon came into its own again. The reading of the Bible was accompanied by the preaching of the Bible. Pulpits were set up in parish churches which had long been without them, and the preaching of the Word became not only a characteristic feature of Reformed Christianity but also a powerful weapon in the propagation of its message.

CHRISTIANITY AND PREACHING

'With preaching,' wrote P. T. Forsyth, 'Christianity stands or falls, because it is the declaration of a Gospel.'[1] There is a sense in which preaching is peculiar to the Christian religion. Certainly it is a characteristic of Christianity in a way in which it is not characteristic of other religions. This is because preaching is bound up with the unique nature of Christianity itself—with what Professor H. H. Farmer has described as 'the sheerly objective, historical, underived givenness which the Christian revelation claims

[1] P. T. Forsyth: *Positive Preaching and the Modern Mind* (London, 1907), p. 5.

for itself. It claims to rest on something unique, decisive, critical which God Himself did "for us men and for our salvation". Its fundamental dogma, in which all other dogmas are implicitly contained, is that in Jesus Christ God came into human history, took flesh and dwelt amongst us, in a revelation of Himself, which is unique, final, completely adequate, wholly indispensable for man's salvation. It all begins in an Event, or rather The Event, God's Event.'

He goes on to say: 'An event can only establish itself —by happening, by being given. And it can only become generally known by being borne witness to, by being proclaimed, by the story being told. The more unparalleled it is, the more, obviously, this is so.' He adds: 'From the beginning, then, Christianity, being concerned with The Event which by definition has no parallel, God being agent in it as He is not in other happenings, was committed to preaching, to proclamation. Whoso said Christianity, said preaching. There was no choice between that and absolutely ceasing to be, with not the least chance of ever occurring again.'[2]

In keeping with this is Dr. Karl Barth's insistence that the fixed point from which all preaching starts is the fact that God has revealed Himself, that everything has already been accomplished. The Word has become flesh; through the death of Christ sin has been dealt with; in Him man has been redeemed once and for all.[3]

All this serves to emphasize not simply the important place, or even the essential place, but the *primary* place

[2] H. H. Farmer: *The Servant of the Word* (London, 1941), pp. 17–19.
[3] Karl Barth: *Prayer and Preaching* (London, 1964), p. 70f.

of preaching in relation to the Christian revelation. The priority of preaching is a vital element in the Reformed tradition in which Anglicanism stands. In a recent series of Warrack Lectures a Presbyterian divine has expressed this conviction in a refreshingly clear and outspoken manner. 'We of the Reformed Church believe that in the true Kirk the pulpit comes first. That is how we understand God's direction to us in Scripture. We can find no authority for laying the emphasis elsewhere. The pulpit comes first. Not the communion table. Not the halls. Not the works of necessity and mercy. But the pulpit. The pulpit is central. The whole life of the congregation turns on the message God gives to us. Preaching first; all else that is helpful afterward. That is the right order.'[4]

THE RESPONSIBILITY OF THE CLERGY

Some no doubt would regard such a statement as an exaggeration. Maybe it is a healthy exaggeration and a needful corrective for our day. At any rate the question must be asked: Is preaching today being given its due recognition by the Church at large, and in the churches of the Anglican Communion in particular? Do the clergy regard it seriously and give it priority?

We can scarcely deny, I think, that broadly speaking preaching is suffering from something of an eclipse; and this is reflected, I would suggest, in the widespread ignorance of the laity. Most of them hear plenty of sermons—of a sort. But what sort? Too many of them are the kind of thing the late Bishop Christopher Chavasse dismissed as 'pitiable little homilies', without much biblical

[4] Hamish C. Mackenzie: *Preaching the Eternities* (Edinburgh, 1963), p. 25.

content or teaching value or converting power. The modern pulpit traffics in snippets of sermons, based on snippets of texts and dealing chiefly with current political or social issues or the latest theological and liturgical eccentricities. It is not by such 'preaching' that converts are won or the people of God built up in their most holy faith.

The laity are hardly to be blamed for their ignorance of the Bible and of Christian doctrine if they have to endure this sort of pulpit ministry Sunday by Sunday. Far from being blamed, they are to be pitied. The blame lies at the door of the ordained ministry. The laity have a right to expect something better of their ministers than this. And they should demand it.

Even a superficial glance at the Ordinal will make it clear that whatever else he is or does, the man ordained to the Anglican ministry is intended to be a preacher. Again and again reference is made to the duty of teaching the faith and of feeding the hungry souls of men with the living Word of God. Take for example these words from the opening part of the Bishop's charge in the Ordering of Priests: 'We exhort you, in the Name of our Lord Jesus Christ, that you have in remembrance into how high a dignity, and to how weighty an office and charge ye are called: that is to say, to be messengers, watchmen, and stewards of the Lord.'

Each of the three titles employed here is eloquent in relation to the preaching office. *Messengers* are those entrusted with tidings to pass on to others. *Watchmen* are the guardians of the safety of the people in their care. *Stewards* are trustees with a responsibility for someone else's goods. Hence the ministers of Christ are charged with the threefold task of passing on His good news to the world, of warning sinners of their danger, and of faithfully dispensing the revealed truth of God to His people.

Look again at the Ordinal. Immediately after the laying on of hands, and in immediate association with it, there takes place an additional ceremony of unmistakable significance. The bishop places in the hand of each newly ordained priest, while still kneeling, a copy of the Bible, with the solemn charge: 'Take thou authority to preach the Word of God, and to minister the holy Sacraments in the Congregation, where thou shalt be lawfully appointed thereunto.'

This is a special feature of the Anglican Ordinal. In the medieval Church it was not the Bible but the communion vessels that were handed to the priest as the traditional 'instruments' of his sacred office. The implication was that the priest was to be first and foremost the servant of the sacrament. The change brought about in 1552 introduced a new conception of the ministry. The ordained priest was to be first and foremost the servant of the Word. The Bible was to have primary place in his life and work. 'Here is symbolism pregnant with meaning,' comments the Archbishop of York. 'Thus the sacred trust is handed on from age to age. Nothing other than the Bible is put into the candidate's hand. It is for him to hold the sacred deposit, to grasp it even more firmly and to expound it ever more faithfully.'[5]

It can certainly be claimed in the light of the Ordinal that our church recognizes the priority of preaching.

But this further question must be faced. Does preach-

[5] Donald Coggan: *Stewards of Grace* (London, 1958), p. 51.

ing count for as much in our day as in past ages? Have not the circumstances of modern life considerably diminished its importance and to some extent rendered it superfluous? So it is sometimes asserted. But the arguments produced are scarcely convincing.

For example, we are often told that this is not an age of great preaching: that we no longer have the pulpit giants of the past—men of the stature of Latimer, Donne, Whitefield, Spurgeon, Liddon, and so on—and that therefore we cannot expect preaching to exert the same commanding influence as of old.

Further, it is pointed out that in this scientific era there are other and more effective means of propagating the Christian message than preaching: that radio, television, films, books, and literature in general are now the recognized media of communication, and that preaching is out-dated, old-fashioned, little more than a rather quaint ecclesiastical anachronism.

Once again, at the present time liturgy is all the fashion and is the chief focus of interest. We are told that worship must come first; that worship is the Church's first duty and is more important than preaching; that people do not go to church to listen to sermons but to give glory to God; that the Parish Communion movement has come to stay and affords little scope for preaching of the old style; and that in any case the modern congregation cannot stand more than five or ten minutes of sermonizing.

This line of reasoning—if it can be dignified by such a name—will not stand up to serious investigation. It reflects an astonishing amount of misunderstanding and muddled thinking. It may possibly afford some measure of comfort to the discouraged parson who has lost his zest for the ministry of the Word and has long since abandoned any attempt to give priority to preaching. But the arguments adduced, when critically examined, are found to be worthless and invalid. In particular they fail to take account of the true nature of preaching: its deeply personal character, its dynamic relation to the saving act of God in Christ, and its abiding place in the purpose of God for His Church in every age.

For what is preaching? That question must now be squarely faced. It is the subject of our next chapter.

CHAPTER TWO

WHAT IS PREACHING?

'SINCE, in the wisdom of God, the world did not know God through wisdom, it pleased God through the folly of what we preach to save those who believe. For Jews demand signs and Greeks seek wisdom, but we preach Christ crucified, a stumbling-block to Jews and folly to Gentiles, but to those who are called, both Jews and Greeks, Christ the power of God and the wisdom of God' (I Cor. 1:21–24).

It is inevitable that in a book about preaching, however simple and unpretentious, these burning words of the apostle Paul should be quoted. They make clear what preaching is and what preaching does. It is a proclamation of Christ and Him crucified, and it is an instrument God uses for man's salvation. True, that which is preached (the *kerygma*) is folly in the eyes of the worldly-wise, as represented by the Greeks, and a stumbling-block to the self-righteous, as represented by the Jews; but to those who by faith respond to God's call—whoever they be—the Gospel of the cross vindicates itself as both the wisdom and the power of God.

What Paul thus wrote to the Church at Corinth was based on his own experience as a preacher. Furthermore, the Corinthians on their part could attest the truth of his words; for they themselves, lowly and despised people as they were, had found in the Christ whom Paul had preached a power which had lifted them to a new level of living, and a wisdom which had imparted to them righteousness and sanctification and redemption (see I Cor. 1:26-32).

SOME DEFINITIONS OF PREACHING

Against this background we may now examine further the question, What is preaching? A great many definitions and explanations have been offered. Probably none is complete or adequate in itself, but it is likely that all have something of value to teach.

Perhaps the shortest and simplest definition is that of Bishop Phillips Brooks—'the communication of truth by man to men'.[1] This conception of preaching as 'the bringing of truth through personality' may not take us the whole way, but it is nevertheless helpful. It reminds us at the outset that preaching is concerned with the *truth*. The truth of course is not ours, it is God's. But preaching is also concerned with *personality*—and that assuredly *is* ours. What is more, personality is an important factor in preaching. It is sheer nonsense to assert that preaching is concerned only with the truth of God and that human personality does not enter into it. In preaching God uses the agency of human persons to convey His message and effect His purpose. The personality of the preacher may help or hinder that purpose; but it cannot be effaced. It has been claimed that personality is the greatest force in the universe. Certainly the power of personality is enormous, and consecrated personality is the most powerful of all.

[1] Bishop Phillips Brooks: *Lectures on Preaching* (London, 1895), p. 5.

Professor Farmer is emphatic that 'preaching is only to be rightly understood and conducted when it is seen in the context of a Christian understanding of persons and their relationships with one another. It is first, last, and all the time a function of the personal world.[2] Hence preaching may be conceived of as God in action through human personality. It has, as Karl Barth insists, a dual aspect: the Word of God and human speech.[3] 'It is the occasion of encounter,' says Thomas Keir in his Warrack Lectures. 'It is a man speaking in such a way and under such a direction that the God who is eternal may be heard to utter His solving and saving Word in the situation that is contemporary.'[4]

This may serve to introduce Bernard Manning's intriguing definition of preaching. He described it as 'a manifestation of the Incarnate Word, from the written Word, by the spoken word'.[5] Whatever be the deficiencies of that definition, it does at least serve to focus attention on two facts of fundamental importance. The first is that the preacher's supreme (and, in one sense, only) theme is Jesus Christ, the incarnate Son, who took our nature that He might bear our sin. The second is that the preacher's authoritative textbook is the Holy Scriptures of the Old and New Testaments. In other words, he not only preaches Christ; he preaches the Christ of revelation. Martin Luther, in quoting the words of the psalmist, 'In the volume of the book it is written of me', inquired, 'What book, and what person?' His answer was: 'There is only

[2] H. H. Farmer: *op. cit.*, p. 36.
[3] Karl Barth: *op. cit.*, p. 65.
[4] Thomas Keir: *The Word in Worship* (London, 1962), p. 121.
[5] Bernard L. Manning: *A Layman in the Ministry* (London, 1943), p. 138.

one book—the Bible. There is only one person—Christ.' For the preacher that answer is of profound significance.

Manning's definition has one other value. It makes clear in what sense preaching is the Word of God. In its primary sense that Word is of course Christ Himself, the incarnate Word. In its secondary sense it is the Bible, the written Word. Hence in a tertiary sense it is the sermon, the preached Word. The word of the preacher becomes the Word of God because he points away from himself to the Bible and the Christ to whom it bears witness.

Preaching is indissolubly bound up with the Gospel. It is not simply the proclamation of the Gospel. It is, in Forsyth's famous phrase, 'the Gospel prolonging and declaring itself'.[6] The Gospel is the good news of the mighty acts of God for man's redemption; the preaching of the Gospel makes those mighty acts a present and urgent reality. 'Through preaching and the response of faith evoked through interpretation of the hearer's environment and experience in the light of the Kerygma, the saving act of God at Calvary becomes a saving act of God now.'[7]

'Preaching,' remarks Dr. R. H. Mounce, 'is that timeless link between God's great redemptive Act and man's apprehension of it.'[8] In thinking of preaching in this light it is essential to recognize that the 'redemptive Act' itself is a fully accomplished work, firmly rooted in the history of the past. As James Denney wrote, 'The work of reconciliation, in the sense of the New Testament, is a work which is *finished*, and which we must conceive to be

[6] P. T. Forsyth: *op. cit.*, p. 5.

[7] D. W. Cleverley Ford: *A Theological Preacher's Notebook* (London, 1962), p. 24.

[8] R. H. Mounce: *The Essential Nature of New Testament Preaching* (Grand Rapids, 1960), p. 153.

finished, *before the gospel is preached*.'[9] But while the preaching of the cross is not in any sense a crucifying of the Son of God afresh, it is an attempt to bring the finished work of the past into the realm of present experience by 'placarding' Christ crucified before the eyes of men (see Gal. 3: 1, Greek).

The character of Christian preaching and its essential content are thus made clear. But what about the *demand* it makes upon its hearers? At this point there is value in Dr. G. Campbell Morgan's definition: 'Preaching is the declaration of the grace of God to human need on the authority of the Throne of God; and it demands on the part of those who hear that they show obedience to the thing declared.'[10] In preaching, as we have been reminded, God is in action through the personality of the preacher; but His action does not end there. It is continued in the hearts and minds and wills of the hearers, who by the grace of the Holy Spirit are enabled to respond in repentance, faith and obedience.

THE FUNDAMENTAL NATURE OF PREACHING

We are now in a position to summarize the fundamental nature of Christian preaching. We can do so quite simply by noting the following four points.

1. First and foremost preaching is wrapped up with the content of the Christian message, the *kerygma*, the divine revelation in Christ. It is the Gospel in action, proclaimed and prolonged, confronting men with God's succour and demand; and since the Gospel has no mean-

---

[9] James Denney: *The Death of Christ* (London, 1902), p. 144f.
[10] G. Campbell Morgan: *Preaching* (London, 1937), p. 15.

ing apart from Christ, preaching centres in the person of the Son of God, the incarnate Word.

2. This at once directs our attention to the place of the Bible in preaching. The Bible as the Word of God written is the record of the divine revelation. Hence, while it is true that the preacher's supreme theme is Christ, not the Bible, in the last analysis he cannot preach Christ apart from the Bible. For the preacher, as for the Church, there is no Christ apart from the Bible.

3. Preaching is not a mechanical process. God does not use automatons to accomplish the task. He uses persons. Since, to recall the words of Karl Barth, preaching has a dual aspect, the Word of God and human speech, so 'God makes use, according to His good pleasure, of the ministry of a man who speaks to his fellow men, in God's name, by means of a passage from Scripture.'[11] Preaching then is a personal activity. This is in accordance with God's revealed method of encountering human souls. All His dealings with men are through men — that is, through the medium of human relationships.

4. The remaining aspect of the subject which needs to be stressed is the role of the persons towards whom the saving activity of God through preaching is directed. Preaching does not take place in a vacuum, nor is it a purely detached, intellectual presentation of truth. It involves a congregation as well as a preacher, and it asks for a verdict. So if the beginning of preaching is the fact that God has spoken and revealed Himself in Christ, the end of preaching is the fulfilment of that revelation in the actual redemption of human life in Christ.[12] And that only

[11] Karl Barth: *op. cit.*, p. 65.
[12] See Karl Barth: *op. cit.*, pp. 70f.

happens when men not only hear the Gospel but receive it and believe it and so embrace the salvation of God (see I Cor. 15:1, 2).

THE PREACHER

These considerations enable us to appreciate the various terms in which the New Testament speaks of the office of a preacher. It is not my purpose to attempt a detailed examination of such terms. This has been done in many of the larger works on preaching, and recently by John Stott in his admirable New Testament word studies entitled *The Preacher's Portrait*.[13]

There are two or three terms which are of particular concern to us. The ordinary Greek word rendered 'to preach' (*keryssein*) means to proclaim as a herald; hence the word we have already met with, *kerygma*, the proclamation, the thing preached; and also *keryx*, the preacher or herald himself. It is important to note that the word *keryx* implies an authoritative proclamation. The Grimm-Thayer *Greek-English Lexicon of the New Testament* defines the *keryx* as a herald or a messenger 'who conveyed the official messages of kings, magistrates, princes, military commanders', and remarks that the verb *keryssein* always carries with it the suggestion of 'an authority which must be listened to and obeyed'.

Another New Testament word used for preaching is *euangelizesthai*, to preach good tidings. In the Christian context it means, of course, to proclaim the Evangel, the good news of God and His redeeming grace. The emphasis here is upon the content of the message preached.

A third word is *oikonomos*, a steward, a person to whom

[13] J. R. W. Stott: *The Preacher's Portrait* (London, 1961).

the head of a household delegates responsibility and entrusts the management of his affairs. It is the word used by St. Paul in I Corinthians 4:1 where he urges his readers to have a right conception of the Christian ministry. 'This is how one should regard us,' he writes, 'as servants of Christ and stewards of the mysteries of God. Moreover, it is required of stewards that they be found trustworthy.' These last words bring out the essential idea involved in stewardship, namely faithfulness in dealing with the master's goods.

In the case of the Christian preacher the 'goods' entrusted to him are 'the mysteries of God'. The word *mysteries*—so often found in the Pauline epistles—refers not to something which cannot be understood, but to things which are beyond human discovery and which can only be known as they are revealed by God Himself. The revelation has taken place—in Christ. So the mysteries of God are His open secret, 'the sum total of His self-revelation which is now embodied in the Scriptures. Of these revealed "mysteries" the Christian preacher is the steward, charged to make them further known to the household'.[14]

Together the three words at which we have been looking paint a clear and unmistakable picture. They delineate the Christian preacher as a man with an authority, a man with a message, and a man with a responsibility. His authority is that of the throne of heaven; his message is God's good news concerning Jesus Christ; and his responsibility is that of safeguarding and sharing the truth which God Himself has made known.

There is one further word—and a word which particularly concerns us in this study—which epitomizes and

[14] J. R. W. Stott: *op. cit.*, p. 19.

combines these ideas. It is the word *ambassador* (Greek *presbus*). The preacher of the Gospel is an ambassador for Christ. St. Paul, in writing to the Corinthians about the ministry of reconciliation entrusted to him by God, says: 'We come therefore as Christ's ambassadors. It is as if God were appealing to you through us: in Christ's name, we implore you, be reconciled to God' (II Cor. 5:20, N.E.B.).

An ambassador is the official representative of his sovereign or government. He is charged with authority by those who send him and has the full right to speak and act on their behalf. There could be no more appropriate word to apply to the preacher of Christ's Gospel. It magnifies his office and invests him with a heavenly dignity. It makes clear that the Christian ambassador is someone to be reckoned with. He is not a mere nobody. In himself he may be feeble and fallible enough, but when he speaks for God to men he does so as an envoy of the King of kings. 'As earthly kings are represented by their ambassadors,' wrote Charles Simeon, 'and speak by them in foreign courts, so the Lord Jesus Christ Himself speaks by His ministers. They stand in His stead; they speak in His name; their word is not their own but His, and must be received "not as the word of man, but as it is in truth, the word of God".'[15]

THE PREACHER'S AUTHORITY

From this it is clear that authentic Christian preaching should be distinguished by the note of *authority*. If indeed those who are called to the ministry of the Word are

---

[15] From his sermon on 'The Excellency of the Liturgy'.

'ambassadors on behalf of Christ' and speak in Christ's stead, it ill befits them to declare God's message in a servile, apologetic, deferential manner, in doubtful and uncertain tones. 'God wants no grovelling, faint-hearted creatures for His ambassadors,' writes Professor James Stewart: 'He wants men who, having communed with heaven, can never be intimidated by the world.' And how true it is, as he goes on to declare, that 'the preacher across whose consciousness that thrilling word—"in Christ's stead"—has pealed needs no other apostolic succession to invest him with the insignia of authority. He is not diffidently offering men the dubious results of his private speculation: he is standing on his feet to deliver to them, in the name of the King of kings, a word that cannot return void.'[16]

This note of spiritual authority derives directly from the preacher's divine commission as Christ's ambassador, as a man sent from God, as well as from the character of his message as the eternal Gospel of the grace of God, rooted in historical events and centred in the unchanging Christ. Moreover, this authoritative note is all the more an urgent necessity in the days in which we live. The world is in a state of bewildered uncertainty. But more: there is theological and moral confusion in the Church itself. It is tragic that men who profess to be the ministers of the Gospel appear to be more sure of what they do not believe than of what they do. They are convinced of their doubts; they are doubtful of their convictions. But the final tragedy is that instead of keeping their miserable doubts to themselves they drag them into the pulpit and give them an airing in almost every sermon. There is no

[16] James S. Stewart: *Heralds of God* (London, 1946), pp. 212, 214.

apostolic 'We know!' about their preaching but only a hesitant 'We venture to suggest'.

Speculation is not preaching. Speculation will never win a verdict for Christ, or advance the kingdom, or meet the cravings of the human heart. Inherent in man's nature is the longing for certainty. 'Give me the benefit of your convictions, if you have any,' remarked Goethe. 'Keep your doubts to yourself; I have enough of my own.'

In the days before the last war, when the reign of liberal theology was at its height, that doughty and fearless Methodist preacher, Dr. Dinsdale T. Young, drew packed congregations to the Central Hall, Westminster, to listen to the old-fashioned Gospel. Among those who were frequently seen in the congregation was a certain high court judge. When asked why he chose to listen to Dinsdale Young instead of to preaching of a more intellectual and fashionable kind, he answered, 'When I go to church I like to hear affirmations.'

Christian preaching is concerned with affirmations. It is based on revelation, not on speculation. It is positive, not negative. Its characteristic is an exclamation mark, not a question mark. Its keynote is 'Thus saith the Lord!' Is it not high time we got this authoritative, dogmatic note back into our preaching? In saying that, I am not suggesting for one moment that we should preach in a proud, boastful, arrogant manner. Nor would I deny that there *are* real problems to be faced, or pretend that the Christian has all the answers. God forbid that we should ever be lacking in humility! All our boast is in the Gospel, not in ourselves. 'We have this treasure in earthen vessels,' as St. Paul reminded the Corinthians, 'to show that the transcendent power belongs to God and not to us' (II Cor.

4 : 7). For as the apostle had already reminded his readers, 'We preach not ourselves, but Jesus Christ as Lord, with ourselves as your servants for Jesus' sake' (v. 5). Ourselves —*servants*; and servants are lowly people. That is the kind of people God would have His ambassadors to be. Like John the Baptist, we are obliged to say of our Blessed Lord, 'He must increase, but I must decrease' (Jn. 3 : 30).

The man who is truly humble, who makes little of himself and much of Christ, will for that very reason preach with burning sincerity and spiritual passion. His whole heart will be in the business. Preaching which is devoid of passion is hardly the genuine Christian thing. This is not a matter of mere excitement, of getting feverishly worked up and becoming artificially emotional. It is all too easy for a sermon to be more marked by perspiration than by inspiration. But when the fire of God's love burns in a man's soul he will find it difficult to speak without force and fervour. The calm detached manner of the lecture hall does not well become the Christian pulpit. Let us be criticized if need be for our lack of learning or polish or eloquence, but not for our lack of earnestness or enthusiasm. If our preaching fails to catch fire, it will hardly warm the hearts of our hearers. In fact, it will simply leave them cold. And that is the effect which so much preaching seems to produce.

'Half the sermons today — may I be forgiven if I am cruel — are failing because they lack the note of passion,' wrote Campbell Morgan,[17] who recalled the story told about the great English actor, Macready. An eminent preacher once asked him this question: 'What is the reason for the difference between you and me? You are

[17] G. Campbell Morgan: *op. cit.*, p. 54.

appearing before crowds night after night with fiction, and the crowds come wherever you go. I am preaching the essential and unchangeable truth, and I am not getting any crowd at all.'

Macready answered, 'This is quite simple. I can tell you the difference between us. I present my fiction as though it were truth; you present your truth as though it were fiction.'

Preaching is at once a test and a demonstration of a man's sincerity. It reveals how much the truth he preaches means to him: how far he is not simply master of his subject but is mastered by it. There is no great preaching that is without the note of passion. St. Paul reminded the Ephesian elders that during the three years of his Asian ministry he 'did not cease night and day to admonish every one with tears' (Acts 20:31). Doubtless his tears added force to his admonition. Jesus wept over Jerusalem. Do we ever weep for the souls of men—and preach as though we had done so? 'O sirs,' cried Richard Baxter, 'how plainly, how closely and earnestly should we deliver a message of such a nature as ours is, when the everlasting life or death of men is concerned in it. . . . Such a work as preaching for men's salvation should be done with all our might—that the people can feel us preach when they hear us.' [18]

One other mark of true Christian preaching must be mentioned, and that is *clarity*. It was Archbishop Magee who made the remark that there are three classes of sermons: those you cannot listen to, those you can listen to, and those you cannot help listening to. Sermons of this third order—sermons which really grip the attention of the

[18] From *The Reformed Pastor* (London, 1950), p. 106.

congregation—are not ambiguous and incomprehensible but clear, simple, and objective in character.

Obscurity is one of the fatal enemies of the pulpit. And it is here, I am persuaded, that not a little of modern preaching falls short. The man in the pew derives no benefit from it—not because he doesn't believe it but because he can't understand it. This may be due to the fact that the sermon is dealing with some obscure theme beyond the range of his interest or intelligence. Or it may be due to the fact that the sermon is couched in high-sounding theological jargon which makes no more sense to him than would Hindustani. There are preachers who indulge in a pseudo-intellectuality and appear to take a special delight in bewildering their hearers by a display of verbal gymnastics. It is a sorry sort of business. To make easy things hard, it has been observed, is any man's job; but to make hard things easy is the work of a great preacher.

This failure to achieve clarity in the pulpit may not be due to the preacher being too much of a scholar to enable him to get down to the level of ordinary folk. Far from it. Some of the most distinguished and popular preachers of our own day are men of high academic standing. It would be flattering in the extreme to many a preacher to suggest that he has thought so deeply about his subject that he cannot find simple and straightforward language in which to express it! The truth in all likelihood is that he has not thought about the subject enough—not enough, that is, to clarify it in his own mind, and therefore not enough to make it luminous to his congregation.

Let it be said quite plainly that we have not really understood *anything* until we have reached the point where we can explain it, without recourse to jargon, to people with no previous knowledge of the subject. This is a searching test indeed; yet it is a test which every ambassador for Christ is called upon to face quite candidly.

Martin Luther used to say that a preacher ought so to speak that, when the sermon is ended, the congregation should be able to disperse saying, 'The preacher said *this*.' Unless the sermon does convey an explicit message and make a clear impression of that kind, it is a failure. The other ingredients of true preaching which we have mentioned previously—authority, humility, sincerity—are of little value in the end without simplicity.

The task is not easy. But then preaching is never easy. It makes tremendous demands. It calls forth the best a man has to give. Yet how immeasurably worth while it is! It is an amazing privilege to be called to the ministry of the Word; to be conscious of a heavenly mission and authority; to be entrusted with a Gospel which is still the power of God for salvation and is utterly adequate for all the complexities of modern life; to be allowed to point men and women and young people to the only way of life in this world and the only hope for the world to come; to be Christ's ambassadors and fellow-workers with God in the greatest of all tasks—the making of disciples, the building up of the Church, the advancement of the kingdom in the world.

'Seeing then that we have been entrusted with this commission, which we owe entirely to God's mercy, we never lose heart. We have renounced the deeds that men hide for very shame; we neither practise cunning nor distort the Word of God; only by declaring the truth openly do we recommend ourselves, and then it is to the common conscience of our fellow-men and in the sight of God . . .

It is not ourselves that we proclaim; we proclaim Christ Jesus as Lord, and ourselves as your servants, for Jesus' sake. For the same God who said, "Out of darkness let light shine", has caused His light to shine within us, to give the light of revelation—the revelation of the glory of God in the face of Jesus Christ' (II Cor. 4: 1, 2, 5, 6, N.E.B.).

CHAPTER THREE

PREACHING AND THE BIBLE

WHEN in Bunyan's *Pilgrim's Progress* Christian came to the House of the Interpreter he was taken first into a private room, where 'Christian saw the picture of a very grave person hanging up against the wall; and this was the fashion of it: it had eyes lifted up to heaven, the best of books in his hand, the law of truth was written upon his lips, the world was behind its back; it stood as if it pleaded with men, and a crown of gold did hang over its head'.

This is Bunyan's portrait of the evangelical preacher. Every feature of it is instructive. For our present purpose we note the significance of the words, *the best of books in his hand*. The Gospel minister has a firm grasp of the truth —the truth of God revealed in Holy Scripture; and that truth of God is not only in his hand but also upon his lips: 'He stood as if he pleaded with men.'

The Christian preacher is the servant of the Word. He is a man under authority. He is, as John Wesley delighted to describe himself, *homo unius libri*, a man of one book. He is not an originator; he is the custodian of a revelation which has already been given. 'There is, therefore, nothing to be said which is not already to be found in the Scriptures. No doubt the preacher will be conscious of the weight of his own ideas which he drags after him; but ultimately he must decide whether he will allow himself to compromise or whether, in spite of all the notions at the back of his mind, he will accept the necessity of expounding the Book and nothing else.'[1]

THE PREACHER'S TEXTBOOK

The Bible is the preacher's textbook: not in the sense that it is an interesting and handy anthology of 'texts' from which he may select a few choice words on which to hang his discourse, but in the sense that it is the authoritative Word which it is his main business to expound and on which he bases the whole of his message. Only as he looks at the Scriptures in this light will he be able to meet the needs of those to whom he ministers. 'The unspoken cry of every gathered congregation to the preacher is not "Is there any bright idea from the current religious debate?" but "Is there any word from the Lord?"—not "We would see what advice may be available," but "We would see Jesus." '[2] It is this unspoken cry of the human heart that continually drives the preacher back to the Bible to find that word from the Lord.

There are, I believe, three main reasons why from a purely practical point of view the preacher should be a man of the Book. I state them as briefly as possible, without attempting at this point to enlarge upon them.

First of all, because the Bible makes its own strong and direct appeal to the heart of man. Explain it as you may, it is nevertheless true that the Bible speaks to men when all other voices fail. Moreover, it never loses its appeal. To each succeeding generation it speaks afresh, and speaks as no other book does, with spiritual authority.

[1] Karl Barth: *op. cit.*, p. 89.
[2] J. S. Stewart: *A Faith to Proclaim* (London, 1953), p. 29.

It possesses a perennial interest. It exercises an unending fascination. In no sphere does it vindicate itself so mightily as the living and abiding Word of God as in the pulpit.

The second reason is this: because only the Bible is sufficient to keep the preacher going throughout his ministry. If he preaches simply his own ideas, his favourite themes, the passing topics of the hour, he will sooner or later run dry. He will come to the end of his resources. Without wearisome repetition, he will have nothing further to say. But in the Scriptures, with their inexhaustible riches and infinite variety of material, he will find plenty to keep him going so long as time and strength are granted to him.

That brings me to the third reason why the preacher should be a man of one book: because only so will he be able to fulfil his ministry and declare the whole counsel of God. The truth is big, many-sided and all-embracing. Man on the other hand is small and restricted in his outlook. His vision is narrow: he cannot see things whole. This is where the Bible comes to the preacher's aid. It enlarges his horizon. It enables him to see the truth in all its varied aspects and to maintain a balanced ministry. It imparts breadth as well as depth to his preaching.

Biblical preaching proceeds along two main lines which, while they can be distinguished, ought not to be too sharply differentiated. We are accustomed to express these in the two Greek words *kerygma* and *didache*. The first of these refers to the preached Gospel in the more restricted sense, being 'the public proclamation of Christianity to the non-Christian world', while *didache* ('teaching') has to do with the subsequent instruction of an ethical and doctrinal character imparted to the converted.[3]

The difference between the two words and their relation one to another has been the subject of a good deal of inquiry. This need not detain us here. What does concern us is that, broadly speaking, the words *kerygma* and *didache* suggest two types of preaching, evangelistic and expository; and while the two are closely related to one another, and cannot ultimately be separated, it may be helpful at this point to say something about each in turn.

EVANGELISTIC PREACHING

'The good news that thundered across the Roman Empire and brought back hope to a disillusioned world was not prescriptions about Christian conduct: it was "Jesus and the Resurrection". It went out with a victory behind it.'[4] In other words, what the apostles preached to the world was not *didache* but *kerygma*. They told of what God in Christ had done for man's salvation—of sin forgiven, death vanquished, and the kingdom of heaven opened to all believers.

This is the essential note in the Evangel. As Dr. John Mackay has put it, the primary element in the Christian religion is not a great imperative—something man is called upon to do for God—but a great indicative: something God has already done for man. There is indeed a divine imperative which arises out of the Christian Gospel, the call to repentance and faith; but it is secondary, not primary. 'The divine imperative is founded upon a re-

[3] See C. H. Dodd: *The Apostolic Preaching and its Development* (London, 1936), p. 7f.

[4] F. R. Barry: *Faith in Dark Ages* (London, 1940), p. 60f.

demptive act enshrined in a divine indicative.'[5] So then the authentic New Testament Gospel is not 'Do this', or 'Obey these rules', or 'Imitate Jesus Christ'. It is rather, 'Christ died for our sins according to the scriptures.' As it has been said, the primitive *kerygma* is not good advice or good example but good news.

This good news is nowhere epitomized more clearly and concisely than in the familiar words of St. John 3: 16. Here is the beginning, the centre and the end of the Gospel.

God so loved the world that He gave . . . That is how the verse begins, and that is also the beginning of the Gospel. Not our love for God but His for us is the starting point (see I Jn. 4: 9, 19). From a theological point of view this insistence on the primacy of divine grace is all-important. The good news is indeed 'the gospel of the grace of God', as the apostle called it (Acts 20: 24). It proclaims the love of God in action. It affirms that what man did not deserve, and could not do, God has done for him. Regardless of man's due, and mindful only of man's need, God has in infinite love acted decisively for man's redemption.

How was that love expressed? *He gave His only begotten Son* . . . Here is the middle of the verse; and at its very heart we meet with the person of Christ—the Christ of Calvary, the Son of Man 'lifted up' to rescue men from eternal death (see the two preceding verses, which form the background to verse 16). Nothing could be more significant than that, for Christ and Him crucified is central to the Gospel. He is Himself the Gospel, the embodiment

[5] John A. Mackay: *A Preface to Christian Theology* (London, 1942), p. 108.

of the good news, the one in whom the saving grace of God is personified. Christianity is Christ.

And what is the end of the Gospel? *That whosoever believeth in Him should not perish, but have everlasting life.* That word *life* sums up the whole design of the Gospel. It is a rescue operation. Apart from Christ the world is *perishing*. The Gospel faces the grim realities of the human situation. It recognizes the corruption of man's heart, his lostness and hopelessness in himself. And it provides the only answer. It is in fact the good news about God which meets the bad news about man: the good news not only of redemption but of regeneration. So the Gospel, like this remarkable verse, begins with everlasting love and ends with everlasting life.

RECONCILIATION

There are two important passages in St. Paul's Corinthian correspondence which illustrate the nature of evangelistic preaching. In II Corinthians 5: 18–21 the apostle throws light on three matters: on the character of the *evangelist*, as being Christ's ambassador; on the goal of *evangelism*, the reconciling of men to God; and on the substance of the *evangel*, the finished work of the cross. 'God was in Christ reconciling the world to Himself, not counting their trespasses against them, and entrusting to us the message of reconciliation. So we are ambassadors for Christ, God making His appeal through us. We beseech you on behalf of Christ, be reconciled to God. For our sake He made Him to be sin who knew no sin, so that in Him we might become the righteousness of God.'

Reconciliation is one of the big words of the Christian Gospel—'perhaps the most comprehensive single word of the New Testament', as Dr. F. W. Dillistone remarks.[6] It is a word which makes plain the fundamental need of man: to be put right with God, with society, and with himself; and what the apostle is stressing in the passage before us is that this need has been fully met in Christ and simply awaits man's acceptance. Man cannot achieve it: he can only receive it. Why? Because everything has already been done—and done by God. In William Temple's well known words, the only thing that man can contribute to his own redemption is the sin from which he needs to be redeemed.

The 'finished work of Christ' has always been one of the great evangelical emphases, and always will be. Here St. Paul gives expression to it with the utmost boldness of language. *All is from God*, he writes (verse 18), for the initiative lies entirely with Him, the loving Father; and in Christ He has accomplished once for all the reconciling deed for men, *not counting their trespasses against them*. How was that possible? Against whom were the trespasses of men counted? The answer is: *For our sake He made Him to be sin who knew no sin, so that in Him we might become the righteousness of God*.

It is an astonishing statement. If words have any meaning at all, this is substitution. Christ, the Holy One, took our place of condemnation before God in order that we, the guilty ones, might take His place of acceptance before God. He identified Himself with our sin that we might become identified with His righteousness. Yet while we can state the fact as baldly as that, we must acknowledge that here is something infinitely wonderful, beyond our comprehension. ' "Tis mystery all!' as Charles Wesley

[6] F. W. Dillistone: *The Christian Faith* (London, 1964), p. 147.

reminds us in one of his greatest hymns; and we need that reminder, lest we should pretend to knowledge beyond our understanding. But, thank God, it is not mystery only:

> *'Tis mercy all, immense and free;*
> *For, O my God, it found out me!*

And so, as a consequence:

> *No condemnation now I dread;*
> *Jesus, and all in Him, is mine!*
> *Alive in Him, my living Head,*
> *And clothed in righteousness divine,*
> *Bold I approach the eternal throne,*
> *And claim the crown, through Christ, my own.*

This is the ultimate issue of the Gospel. So, in view of all that God has done, the apostle makes an urgent appeal —in fact, a divine appeal: *We beseech you on behalf of Christ, be reconciled to God.* Let it be clearly noted that this is characteristic of evangelistic preaching. As Professor Dodd has pointed out, 'the *kerygma* always closes with an appeal for repentance, the offer of forgiveness and of the Holy Spirit, and the promise of "salvation", that is, of "the life of the Age to Come", to those who enter the elect community.'[7] Examples of such an appeal are to be found in several of the apostolic sermons reported in the Acts (see, for example, 2:38, 39; 3:19; 10:43; 13:38–41).

This means that modern evangelistic preaching which summons men to repentance and faith and urges a personal commitment to Christ is in line with the New Testament message and method. The fact is, the Gospel proclamation and appeal belong together. 'The true herald

[7] C. H. Dodd: *op. cit.*, p. 23.

of God is careful first to make a thorough and thoughtful proclamation of God's great deed of redemption through Christ's cross, and then to issue a sincere and earnest appeal to men to repent and believe. Not one without the other, but both.'[8]

The other Pauline passage to which reference must be made is in I Corinthians 15: 1–11. Here the apostle begins by saying, *I would remind you, brethren, in what terms I preached to you the gospel* (v. 1). So in thought we are taken back to that time in Paul's ministry when at the close of his second missionary journey he came as Christ's ambassador to the city which had the worst reputation of its day for vice and crime—the Vanity Fair of the Roman Empire, as Dean Farrar dubbed it. He came, as he later confessed, 'in weakness and in much fear and trembling'. But he came as the bearer of good tidings: *I delivered to you as of first importance what I also received, that Christ died for our sins in accordance with the scriptures, that He was buried, that He was raised on the third day in accordance with the scriptures.*

We cannot fail to note that Paul's preaching of the Gospel was concerned with solid, objective facts: the death of the cross, the burial in Joseph's tomb, and the resurrection 'on the third day'. The latter phrase securely anchors the Gospel to the realm of time and history. In Paul's reckoning Christ's resurrection was just as much a fact—and a fact of precisely the same nature—as His death and burial. As far as he was concerned, without the resurrection there was no good news. This is the particular point he is making here. The Christ who died and was buried is the Christ who was raised on the third

[8] J. R. W. Stott: *op. cit.*, p. 51.

day; and it was *this* Christ that he and the other apostles had preached (see verse 11).

PREACHING CHRIST

Clearly then to preach the Gospel is to preach Christ. The Gospel *is* 'the Gospel of Christ'. The phrase indicates not only that Christ is the source of the Gospel, the one in whom it originates. It reminds us also that Christ is the theme of the Gospel, its sum and substance. Indeed, as we have already indicated, in the last resort Christ is His own Gospel. While it may be possible to preach Christ without preaching the Gospel, it is quite impossible to preach the Gospel without preaching Christ.

But what does it mean to preach Christ? For a serious and scholarly answer to that question I would draw attention to Professor James Denney's article entitled 'Preaching Christ' in Hastings' *Dictionary of Christ and the Gospels*.[9] In that article he makes clear that to preach Christ is not merely to narrate the history of Jesus in the Gospels but to preach Him in the sovereignty of His resurrection, to preach Him as *One who lives and reigns*.

'It is not preaching Christ if we tell the story of the life and death merely as events in a past continually growing more remote. It is not preaching Christ though we tell this story in the most vivid and moving fashion, and gather round it, by the exercise of historical imagination or dramatic skill, the liveliest emotions; it is not preaching Christ to present the life and death of Jesus as a high and solemn tragedy, with power in it to purify the soul by pity

[9] Hastings: *Dictionary of Christ and the Gospels* (Edinburgh, 1908), Vol. II, pp. 393-403.

and terror. There is no preaching of Christ, possessed of religious significance, that does not rest on the basis on which the apostolic preaching rested: His exaltation in power, and therefore His perpetual presence. The historical Jesus is indispensable; but if we are to have a Christian religion, the historical must become present and eternal. This it does through the resurrection apprehended by faith.'[10]

Denney lays special stress on the *uniqueness* of the Christ who is presented in the Gospel: the uniqueness of His life and death, the uniqueness of His person and claims, and the uniqueness of His place in the Christian revelation. Thus, commenting on the questions raised in I Corinthians, 'What is Apollos? What is Paul? Was Paul crucified for you? or were you baptized in the name of Paul?' he remarks: 'What St. Paul means in the words cited is that any other person has only a relative importance in Christianity, while Christ's importance is absolute. The Church would have missed Paul and Apollos, but it would have been there; whereas but for Christ it could not have been there at all. It existed only *in* Him. This is assumed in all preaching of which He is the object. His significance for the Church is not in the same line with that of Paul and Apollos; it is in the same line with that of the Father.'[11]

Again, referring to St. Paul's explosive language in Galatians 1:8, 9 with regard to the preaching of 'another gospel', Denney comments: 'What these two seemingly intolerant verses mean is that Christ is the whole of the Christian religion, and that to introduce other things side

[10] Hastings: *op. cit.*, p. 394f.
[11] James Denney: *op. cit.*, p. 400.

by side with Him, as if they could supplement Him, or share in His absolute significance for salvation, is treason to Christ Himself. Christ crucified—the whole revelation of God's redeeming love to sinners is there; the sinful soul abandoning itself in unreserved faith to this revelation—the whole of the Christian religion is there. Whoever brings into religion anything else than Christ and faith, as though anything else could conceivably stand on the same plane, is, wittingly or unwittingly, the deadly enemy of the gospel.'[12]

Such a dogmatic and uncompromising view of Christ and the Gospel may not be in harmony with the tolerant and speculative spirit of this age, but it has the advantage of being in line with the witness of the New Testament. To preach the Gospel the evangelist must be sure of the Gospel; and that means he must be sure of Christ. There is no effective evangelism that does not proceed from the apostolic conviction that there is salvation in no one else but the Lord Jesus: that there is no other name under heaven given among men by which we must be saved (see Acts 4:12).

EXPOSITORY PREACHING

To preach the Gospel: to teach the Faith. The difference between these two functions of the pulpit must not, as we have already indicated, be pressed too far, even though the distinction is a real one. In practice *kerygma* and *didache* cannot be stored in separate homiletic compartments. Evangelism which lacks definite doctrinal content is not likely to have much lasting effect. On the other hand, there is also a sense in which all preaching should

[12] Ibid.

be evangelistic in tone. The preacher must come back again and again to the basic truths of the evangel.

The fact is, the preacher is not only an evangelist; he is also a teacher. I cannot accept the view expressed by Dr. Norman Pittenger that the parson functions as a preacher *only* when he proclaims Christ, and that he is not to look upon himself, as far as his preaching office is concerned, as a teacher. 'It is a mistake,' he says, 'to use the *pulpit* for what we might describe as didactic purposes, however important and necessary the task of teaching may be in other connections.'[13]

There is, admittedly, a danger lest the pulpit be abused and the sermon become a mere lecture. Preaching which is purely academic readily degenerates into a dry-as-dust exposition. And I agree with the comment: 'Such exposition can be very dull if it is only a statement of dead certainties. The dead certainties must come alive, must glow, pulsate, move, speak to the urgencies and pressures of workaday life. Divinity must be humanized.'[14]

There is teaching which has a deadening effect, and likewise there is teaching which is instinct with life. The Christian preacher will strive to the utmost to ensure that the teaching he imparts from the Word of God is of this latter sort.

There is really no such thing as non-doctrinal preaching. All Christian proclamation must have some theological content if it is a genuine unfolding of the divine revelation and of the redemption which is in Christ Jesus. It is said

---

[13] W. Norman Pittenger: *Proclaiming Christ Today* (London, 1963), p. 5.

[14] Arthur A. Cowan: *The Primacy of Preaching To-day* (Edinburgh, 1955), p. 85.

that when Dr. R. W. Dale was appointed to his church in Birmingham he was warned that the congregation would not stand doctrinal sermons. 'They'll have to stand them!' was his reply. And they did stand them for the forty years of Dr. Dale's distinguished ministry at Carr's Lane Chapel.

The expounding of doctrine is not the only kind of teaching required of the preacher. Other subjects will also find their place in the syllabus. Christian *ethics* certainly come within the sphere of the preacher's ministry, as the New Testament epistles forcibly remind us. It is remarkable how large a proportion of the epistles is devoted to the task of relating the Christian faith to ordinary, everyday things, the concrete realities of Christian living. I shall have something further to say about this in the final chapter. The principles of Christian *worship* constitute another important theme for preaching; and this will include clear sacramental teaching. I need hardly add that from our Anglican point of view it is right and proper that we should relate such teaching to the Book of Common Prayer, and also use the Prayer Book to illustrate the various aspects of Christian liturgy.

Doctrine, morals, worship—these are the main matters about which teaching is required; and they are all essentially *biblical* matters. This means in the end that expository preaching in the best sense of the term must be characterized by biblical exposition. It is not enough that the teaching given be simply based on the Bible and in general harmony with its message. The teaching must emerge directly from the Bible and should in fact be the expounding of a Bible passage. This is something entirely different.

I would make a special plea for expository preaching of this type as distinct from what is usually called 'textual' preaching on the one hand and 'topical' preaching on the other. In much *textual* preaching the text in question may not be of fundamental importance to the sermon as a whole. It may be little more than a few odd words of Scripture torn from the context and used as a suitable starting point for the sermon or as an illustration of its general theme. That is not what I mean by expository preaching. *Topical* preaching is even further removed from it. There is no doubt a place for such preaching, as for example when some burning issue of the day clamours for attention from the pulpit. But it must not be overdone. Topical preaching is inclined to wear very thin, and soon loses its appeal.

Expository preaching on the other hand is something more substantial. For that very reason, of course, it can readily become very heavy! The preacher must guard against this. It is his job to make the Bible come alive and allow it to speak to his hearers with power as the contemporary Word of God. If he is to achieve this end he must first wrestle with the passage in question until he has grasped its meaning and been gripped by its message; then he must set about the task of presenting it to his people in such a way that it will be meaningful for them and will speak to their condition. He will not attempt to give them everything that he himself has found in the passage. It is a mistake to try to teach too much at once and to overburden the message. He will rather select from the passage the particular teaching that he feels is going to meet the need of the moment; and, keeping the actual congregation always in mind, he will put across the message he has for them in a clear, simple, vivid fashion, illustrating it in whatever way may be necessary—from life, from nature, from history, from biography, or from the Bible itself—and applying it directly to their own lives and circumstances.

THE DEMANDS OF EXPOSITORY PREACHING

The expounding of a particular part of Holy Scripture in such a manner as this is, I believe, the most effective way of imparting Christian teaching on matters of faith and life and conduct. Needless to say, no single passage of the Bible—and no single sermon—can cover the whole of any one subject. That is especially true of the big doctrines such as the incarnation, the atonement, the resurrection, the Church, the life to come. The same is true of other themes, such as the Christian view of marriage, or the use of money, or the missionary obligation, or race relations, and so on.

But that is all to the good. I can only repeat that it is a fatal mistake to attempt to say too much in one sermon. The wise preacher will be content to deal with one aspect of the matter at a time. 'Precept upon precept, line upon line, here a little, there a little'—such is the teacher's rule. If more complete treatment of a subject is required, then a course of sermons must be planned.

Preaching of this kind is not easy. Any serious ministry of the Word makes considerable demands upon the preacher. First and foremost it demands a real love for the Bible and a profound reverence for its authority. The preacher will get nowhere without that. But more. Expository preaching also demands patient and prolonged study of the Scriptures. The man who is going to preach the Bible must *know* the Bible. He must have a firm, intelligent grasp of its contents and teaching. Paradoxically, if the preacher is to be a servant of the Word he must also become a master of the Word. It is only as the Bible is deeply written in his heart and mind, and he has it so to speak at his finger tips, that he will be able to teach it in such a way as to make it a living book to others.

This means that the preacher must be prepared to do some hard thinking and serious reading—not just spasmodically but as a matter of course. His preaching of the Bible will compel him to have constant recourse to his library: to commentaries, dictionaries, lexicons and other works of biblical reference.

Such study is necessary for two reasons. On the one hand it must be done in order to stimulate his thinking, to sharpen his wits, so that he has something more than the most commonplace sort of comments on the Bible to offer to his congregation. It is necessary on the other hand to ensure that he has an accurate understanding of the passage he is dealing with and interprets it aright. Unfortunately it is only too possible to misinterpret the Scriptures. If he is not careful the preacher may, quite unwittingly, make the Bible say something which it does not say at all.

In this connection I cannot forbear to relate P. T. Forsyth's story about a certain theological seminary in the United States where it was the custom, on a Monday morning, for the students to attend a homiletic class and for each to give a brief account of the sermon he had preached the previous day. On one such occasion the professor of homiletics said to a student, 'What text did you take last night?'

He answered, 'My text was, "How shall we escape if we neglect so great salvation?"'

'A splendid text,' remarked the professor. 'Tell us how you treated it.'

'I didn't try to treat it,' he answered. 'I simply took the two obvious points.'

'And what were they?'

'First, the greatness of our salvation.'

'Very good. What was the second?'

'A little advice on how to escape if we neglect it.'

Perhaps few of us are likely to misinterpret the Scriptures to that extent. But it is certain that a great many pitfalls may be avoided by the simple process of consulting good commentaries and checking up on points of translation; and in that process much additional light may well be thrown on the sacred text. Above all, the preacher should always remember the importance of paying careful attention to the context of the passage with which he is dealing and of viewing the part in relation to the whole. Scripture interprets Scripture. A firm knowledge of the Bible in its entirety is, in the last resort, the best protection against misinterpretation.

Sufficient has been said to make clear that expository preaching is of a demanding nature. It probably requires more time, more study and more effort than any other kind of preaching. But it has immense gains. It is rewarding for the preacher himself, for it continually drives him to his Bible and keeps him at his studies. It is good for the congregation, for it aims to ground them in the truth of God and so to build them up in their most holy faith.

Above all, it honours the Word of God; and by that I mean not only the Bible, the written Word, but the Lord Christ Himself, the incarnate Word. That assuredly is the ultimate goal of all Christian ministry—not least of the ministry of preaching.

CHAPTER FOUR

PREACHING AND WORSHIP

PREACHING takes place within the context of worship, and there is obviously an intimate and important relation between the two. At the outset we must rid our minds of any idea that preaching and worship are in opposition to one another and make rival claims upon us. In particular we must guard against drawing a false antithesis: of thinking of worship as though it were a divine activity, being directed towards God, while regarding preaching as merely human—a man speaking to his fellow-men. Once such an idea is accepted, the inevitable consequence is to magnify worship and to disparage preaching.

But this whole conception is wrong from beginning to end. Worship and preaching are not contradictory. They are not merely complementary. In the deepest sense they are coterminous, co-extensive. Preaching is an integral and essential part of worship.

That raises the question, What do we mean by worship? Whatever answer we give to that question, we must certainly recognize that worship is a corporate activity on the part of the Church; that it is the giving to the Lord the glory that is His due in response to what He has revealed to us and done for us in Jesus Christ His Son.[1]

Is preaching in conflict with this? How can it be if it

[1] See Oswald B. Milligan: *The Ministry of Worship* (London, 1941), p. 14.

is true to New Testament standards? For the aim of preaching is to set forth the glory of God in His love and majesty, in His holiness and power; to declare the mighty acts He has wrought for us men and for our salvation; to present Jesus Christ in His sovereign right and saving grace as the incarnate, crucified and exalted Son. When that is done, the hearts of the hearers will be lifted up to God in penitence and adoration, in gratitude and hope, in faith and submission. And that is worship.

'If Christianity is indeed the revelation of God, and not the research of man,' writes Professor Stewart: 'if preaching is the proclamation of a message which has come not merely through human lips, but from the deeps of the eternal; if the preacher is sent (in St. Paul's expressive phrase) to "placard" Christ, to declare a Word which is not his own, because it is the Word of God Incarnate—it follows that the attempt to segregate preaching from worship is fundamentally false. The fact is that the sermon is divinely intended to be one of those high places of the spirit where men and women grow piercingly aware of the eternal, and where a worshipping congregation—forgetting all about the preacher—sees "no man, save Jesus only."' [2]

If preaching is thus a genuine element in worship, it can in no sense be regarded as an intrusion into the liturgy. It is all of a piece with the prayers and praises of the Church. 'The ordinary Sunday sermon should not be a purple patch, however splendid, inserted into the formal background of the Liturgy . . . The congregation should not normally be invited to turn their attention from what they have been doing in the service in order to stop and

[2] J. S. Stewart: *Heralds of God*, p. 71f.

listen for twenty minutes to the Vicar talking about something else.'[3] Far from that, the congregation should continue in the attitude of worship during the sermon, and through hearing the Word of God continue to glorify His name.

SERMON AND SACRAMENT

Such is the relation between preaching and worship in general terms. We must now go a step further and inquire into the place of the sermon in the administration of the sacraments.

At his ordination the Anglican priest is charged to be 'a faithful dispenser of the Word of God, and of His holy Sacraments'. What exactly is involved in this dispensing of Word and sacraments, more especially the sacrament of the Lord's supper? Are there two different and disconnected ministries involved here—the ministry of the Word and the ministry of the sacrament? Or is it ultimately a single ministry, namely, the ministry of the Word expressing itself in twofold form through sermon and sacrament?

The latter conception is certainly the correct one. 'There is not the preaching of the Word of God and the sacrament; there is the preaching of the Word of God and the sacrament of the Word of God. That is to say that the Word of God is given to us in two forms: it is both preached and signified, and it becomes valid through this dual testimony.'[4]

Again: 'It is the same Gospel that is preached through

[3] M. R. Newbold in *The Parish Communion* (London, 1937), p. 210.

[4] J.-J. Von Allmen: *Preaching and Congregation* (London, 1962), p. 40.

the Word that is proclaimed through the sacraments . . . It is the same grace, whose revitalizing power is brought to us through prayer and the reading and preaching of the Word, which is conveyed to us through "the sensible signs" in the sacraments. In these respects sacramental worship does not differ from ordinary worship, and under no circumstances should the value of one be set in contrast with the value of the other.'[5]

It must be emphasized that both preaching and the sacraments, as divine means of grace, derive all their efficacy from the Word of God. Just as, apart from the Word, preaching has no spiritual value but is mere talk, so likewise the sacraments, apart from the Word, are but a dumb show, empty signs. Preaching is the Word of God made vocal, the sacraments are the same Word of God made visible. It was for this reason that St. Augustine described the sacraments as *verba visibilia*, visible words, as signs to which the promises of the Gospel are annexed. Those promises, proclaimed in the sermon, are sealed in the sacraments.

Moreover, both preaching and the sacraments have the same aim and function: to be channels by which the blessings of the new covenant in Christ's blood are exhibited, set forth, presented and conveyed to men. How this is so is obvious in the case of the preached Word. In the pulpit the minister points his hearers to Christ and Him crucified and calls upon them to repent and believe, in order that they may be partakers of Christ and His saving grace. The same thing happens when the sacrament of the Lord's supper is administered. 'As often as you eat this bread and drink the cup, you proclaim the Lord's

[5] Milligan: *op. cit.*, p. 73.

death until He comes' (I Cor. 11:26). So the sacrament also preaches the crucified Saviour—not so much in word as in deed, in visible, dramatic action; and those who worthily receive the sacrament by faith (that is, faith in Christ, not in the sacrament) are made partakers of His most blessed body and blood. In the words of Mrs. Rundle Charles's hymn:

> *No gospel like this feast,*
> *Spread for Thy Church by Thee;*
> *Nor prophets nor evangelists*
> *Preach the glad news more free:*
> *All our redemption cost,*
> *All Thy redemption won;*
> *All it has won for us, the lost,*
> *All it cost Thee, the Son.*

The sacraments are both *signs* and *seals* of the new covenant. There is a distinction here which ought to be observed. What it means is well brought out in the words of Dr. A. J. Tait: 'A sign of a gift is not necessarily the seal of its donation, and a seal of donation does not necessarily take the form of a sign of the thing given: but the Christian sacraments are at once the signs and the seals. They both signify and donate, represent and present, exhibit and convey. This is it which distinguishes them from bare signs, and makes them *effectual signs* . . . They are effectual signs in respect of grace, only and solely because of God's appointment. The worthy use of them affects their efficacy as . . . means of grace, but it cannot affect their efficacy as signs of grace and God's good will towards us.'[6]

[6] Arthur J. Tait: *The Nature and Function of the Sacraments* (London, 1917), pp. 41-3.

This leads to a further observation in regard to sermon and sacrament. The fact that the sacraments are effectual signs which donate and convey God's grace does not mean that they automatically *bestow* that grace irrespective of the faith of those to whom they are administered—any more than the sermon, which proclaims and offers the same grace of God, automatically bestows on the hearers the gift of salvation whether they believe or not. In other words, sermon and sacrament operate fundamentally on the same principle. Both bear witness to the availability of God's grace in Jesus Christ. Both convey and present that grace to men. But neither the one nor the other compels acceptance of that which is donated. That is not God's way with men. He extends to them His gifts, but He does not compel acceptance. He knocks at the door, but He does not force an entrance.

This is the teaching of Scripture, and our experience endorses it. We know only too well that it is possible for people to sit under the preaching of the Gospel without believing the good news and receiving it for themselves. Their unbelief does not, of course, invalidate the preaching or deny the efficacy of the Gospel; but it does present a barrier to the grace of God. Hence we must agree that the preaching of the Word is not a mechanical means of salvation. St. Paul appeals to his readers, who have heard the word of reconciliation, 'not to accept the grace of God in vain' (II Cor. 6: 1). When this happens, the offer holds good, for it is God's offer; but men choose to reject the offer, and so deny themselves the grace that might have been theirs.

The same is true in regard to the sacraments. They possess no magical efficacy independent of faith. They do not contain grace in themselves or confer grace automatically (*ex opere operato*). It is possible to accept the sign of the sacrament and not to partake of the thing signified. 'The reception of the thing signified depends on the faith of the receiver, for without faith it cannot be received. But the sacrament is the seal of donation nevertheless. And the receiver who knows this cannot escape the responsibility of this. Man's faith does not make the grace of God. Man's faith does not make the sacrament to be the seal of God's grace. It is the office of faith, in the right use of the sacraments, not to make, but to receive, and to receive by believing—by believing the gift conveyed by the seal, by believing that which is in itself truly objective and independent of faith.' Such, writes the Rev. N. Dimock, was the view of the English Reformers.[7]

THE HOLY COMMUNION

This recognition of the parallel roles of the sermon and the sacraments leads us to consider now the specific place of preaching in the service of holy communion. Since sermon and sacrament correspond to one another and fulfil the same general design, it must be clear that it is entirely right and proper that the celebration of the Lord's supper should be accompanied by a sermon. In fact, it is the one occasion in the Church's worship when a sermon is most required; which is no doubt the reason why in the Anglican Prayer Book precise directions are given for the preaching of the Word in the Communion Office: 'Then shall follow the Sermon.' For the *total* ministry of the Word, both sermon and sacrament are necessary.

[7] N. Dimock: *The Doctrine of the Sacraments* (London, 1908), p. 20.

In his *Preaching and Congregation* Professor von Allmen lays down as one of his theses the following (the italics are his): '*The worship of the Church is not complete unless the sacrament accompanies the sermon; for the sermon has as much need of the sacrament as the sacrament has of the sermon.*'[8] He illustrates this thesis by appealing to our Lord's earthly ministry. In preaching the reality of the kingdom of God, present in Himself, Jesus also demonstrated the presence of the kingdom by His miraculous works. He did not preach without giving visible evidence of what He preached.

This illustration helps us to understand the indissoluble link between sermon and sacrament in the celebration of the Lord's supper. 'Preaching thus guarantees that the sacrament is not a magical act, but an intervention, an action of a free God. As for the sacrament, it guarantees that the sermon is not a mere piece of theorizing about God; it prevents the sermon from becoming the discussion of an idea, rather than being a vital and effective moment in an historical process. In addition it obliges the sermon to remain faithful to its mission: when the table stands prepared beside the pulpit it would be an act of unfaithfulness not to preach Jesus Christ dead and risen for us.'[9]

In view of all this, it is strange, as it is also tragic, that in the history of the Church there has been a persistent tendency either to magnify the sacrament at the expense of the sermon, or the sermon at the expense of the sacrament. When this happens, the inevitable result is an unbalanced conception of Christian worship, while at the

[8] J.-J. Von Allmen: *op. cit.*, p. 40.
[9] J.-J. Von Allmen: *op. cit.*, p. 41.

same time we are plunged into a mass of unhappy and unedifying controversy. A conflict takes place between those who regard themselves as the champions of the 'altar' (the word seems wholly appropriate in the present context) and those who stand forth in reply as the protagonists of the pulpit.

In the primitive Church there was no such tension. The early liturgies make it clear that a sermon was a normal and regular feature of eucharistic worship. But in the Middle Ages there was a radical departure from apostolic Christianity and as a result the character of the Church's worship was distorted. The multiplication of masses, as supposedly possessing meritorious efficacy for the departed as well as for the living, combined with a widespread ignorance on the part of the ordinary clergy, resulted in a lamentable decline in preaching. Religion became a ceremonial system, and the Word of God was largely silenced. Archbishop Cranmer, of course, explains all this in the preface to the Book of Common Prayer.

The Reformation in the sixteenth century brought about a revolutionary change. One of the principal aims of the Reformers was to recover a true balance of sermon and sacrament: to ensure that the Lord's supper was restored to its rightful place as a genuinely congregational and intelligible act of worship, in which the Lord's people participated to the full and in which the Word of God was preached. It is grossly untrue to assert that the sermon was intended to be a substitute for the sacrament. 'The Mass was replaced not by the sermon, but . . . by the full diet of Christian worship, the Lord's supper, with sermon and communion of all the people. The Reformers desired to make both the Word and the sacraments fully accessible to the people; in their minds and teaching there was no contradiction between the two.'[10]

This is simply a matter of historical fact. No doubt it is true that in later ages (that is, after the Restoration) preaching sadly declined, and inevitably the sacrament went down with it; so that by the early part of the eighteenth century the holy communion was largely a neglected ordinance. In most parish churches celebrations took place only about four times a year. John Wesley strongly protested against this neglect and insisted on the duty of weekly communion. It can be claimed that in a true sense the Evangelical Revival was also a sacramental revival. Word and worship came into their own again. The vastly increased numbers of communicants necessitated the starting of early morning communion services. This was an evangelical innovation. The Tractarian Movement which followed also gave prominence to the holy communion; but unfortunately its doctrine of the sacrament, and of the role of the congregation in relation to the sacrament, was not always in accordance with the primitive and apostolic pattern. And the preaching of the Word of God —which is our particular concern here—was not given due emphasis.

What is the situation today? It certainly cannot be said that the sacrament of the Lord's supper is neglected in our modern church life. Celebrations of the holy communion are probably more frequent than ever before. Not only in cathedrals but also in many parish churches a daily communion is now the normal thing. But of course

[10] W. D. Maxwell: *Concerning Worship* (London, 1948), p. 68.

this means that the sacrament is regularly celebrated without the preaching of the Word—and in many cases, I fear, without a congregation. At any rate, it must be admitted that the multiplication of communions does not correspond to a multiplication of worshippers. Many churches have reached the position of more and more celebrations for less and less people, accompanied by fewer and fewer sermons.

To me, as an evangelical churchman, this seems an unsatisfactory situation and a retrograde step. It is a move back towards the solitary masses of medieval times and a non-preaching ministry. We do not really honour the sacrament in this way. And I am very concerned that we *should* honour it. My disquiet arises not from my having a low view of the sacrament but from my having a high view of it as a dominical ordinance. I believe it to be a divinely appointed means of grace for the Church of inestimable value; but I also believe that it must be used aright. History demonstrates clearly enough, as we have seen, that the sacrament can only too readily be subject to abuse.

Let me speak plainly, even at the risk of giving offence. The holy communion ought not to be treated as a sort of fetish, as though it conferred some extraordinary benefit upon man (or upon God) whenever it is celebrated—and as though it were the only true means of grace. This is the impression all too often given. I have a certain amount of sympathy with the laity who write to the church papers and complain that the clergy have a perfect obsession with the holy communion and can hardly talk about anything else. There is, in certain cases at least, an unbalanced outlook which is out of harmony with the New Testament.

In the apostolic quadrilateral referred to in Acts 2:42 the 'breaking of bread' (presumably the Lord's Supper) rightly finds a place; but along with it mention is also made of other matters of vital moment: the teaching imparted by the apostles, the fellowship of the Church, and the common prayers. These are also means of grace which cannot be neglected in an apostolic community. Do those who make such abundant provision for holy communion also supply regular opportunities for Bible study, for united prayer, and for Christian fellowship? 'These ought ye to have done, and not to leave the other undone.'

This is a plea for a sense of proportion and for a more worthy use of the Lord's supper. The latter, as the very title implies, is essentially a *corporate* act of worship, a fellowship meal. It demands the presence of a congregation and it should not normally be administered without the preaching of the Word. Therefore it ought not to be hastily celebrated at some impossible hour of the day when it is known that the Lord's people cannot be present — simply in order to conform to a certain ecclesiastical rule or tradition. Sanctified common sense would suggest that the sacramental ideal might be far better realized by less frequent celebrations at a more reasonable time — for example, on weekday *evenings* — when the Lord's people can be present and when the service can be conducted with unhurried reverence, and include a sermon. This, I would suggest, is the only reasonable and fitting way in this modern age of marking the saints' days and other holy days in the Church's calendar. An evening communion of this kind might well be followed by a fellowship meeting in the church hall and a discussion of the sermon.

Here I would also make a plea in passing for a short sermon to be included in the early morning communion service on Sundays. I recognize that this makes a further demand on the clergy; but surely the sacrament should be honoured by being celebrated in full, according to the Church's own requirement.

What I have been saying here is to a large extent in line with the parish communion movement and also with the modern liturgical movement. The parish communion does seek to involve the congregation in the action of the service; it regards reception of the sacrament as the normal thing; and it includes some sort of ministry of the Word. Since for a large number of church people today this is the only regular occasion when they hear a sermon, it is important that every care should be taken to use this preaching ministry to the best possible advantage.

The sermon at holy communion has its own distinctive character. It best fulfils its function when fully integrated into the service by being based on one of the liturgical Scriptures appointed for the day. This provides a natural opportunity for expository preaching of a simple, devotional kind. Preaching on passing topics or controversial issues is out of place here. What is required is a *sermon*, even though it may be quite brief. A few random and disjointed 'thoughts' on the Epistle or Gospel will certainly not suffice.

The importance of the Church's year is nowhere more marked than in preaching of this kind. The sermon should reflect the spirit and tone of the season: whether it be the solemnity of Advent with its note of judgment, or the gladness of Christmas with its thanksgiving for the Word made flesh, or the hopefulness of the Epiphany season with its witness to the world-wide purpose of God; and so on.

One word of caution arises out of this. Preaching *at* the communion does not necessarily involve preaching *about* the communion. What the preacher is required to do at such a time is not to discourse endlessly on the sacrament but to proclaim the One to whose person and work the sacrament bears constant witness. There is, of course, a place for sacramental teaching from the pulpit; but this will be occasional rather than regular. The preacher's main job is not to preach up the sacraments but rather, like St. Paul, to determine to know nothing but Jesus Christ and Him crucified.

MORNING AND EVENING PRAYER

The Sunday services of morning and evening prayer, though not expressly designed to be themselves preaching services (no sermon is prescribed), offer a particular opportunity for the ministry of the Word. The preacher now is less restricted than at the holy communion. A broader field is open to him. At evensong, when people are less time-conscious than in the morning, the preacher may spread his wings a bit and not feel all the time that he must have one eye on the clock.

About this matter of sermon length, we must be realistic. We are not now living in leisurely Victorian times when the pace of life was not what it is today. Modern church people—at least English ones—are not prepared to endure either long services or long sermons.

There is no reason why they should be asked to do so. Morning and evening prayer are not long services in themselves, but they can be drawn out to an almost unendurable degree by elaborate music, numerous hymns, lengthy intercessions, interminable (and impossibly dull) notices, and so on. When on top of all this—maybe nearly an hour after the service started—there is added a full-blown sermon, the patience of the congregation is tested to breaking-point.

If the preacher is to make the most of the opportunity, he must bear these considerations in mind. But having said that let me add that I write as one who is convinced that the traditional Sunday morning and evening services can still today, with a little trouble and imagination, become acts of living worship; and they certainly afford a splendid background for a vital pulpit ministry. Preaching material is readily available in the appointed lessons from the Old and New Testaments. There is also ample scope for courses of sermons, especially during such seasons as Advent and Lent. The long Trinity season might with profit be used for the same purpose, since during the summer and autumn months subjects can be dealt with which are not altogether appropriate for special seasons of the year.

Courses of sermons have a number of advantages. As far as the preacher himself is concerned, they provide him with a chance of doing some specialized reading and study in connection with the selected topic, and they also enable him to know his sermon themes well in advance—an obvious gain. From the congregation's point of view, such courses not only serve to stimulate interest in the preaching ministry; they also open up new territory and enable regular churchgoers to learn something about subjects which, in the usual course of events, might not be dealt with in the pulpit.

Clearly enough, as we have already indicated, there are some subjects which are too big to be encompassed by just one isolated sermon, and as a result the preacher is inclined to leave them alone. Take, for example, the Ten Commandments. What is the use of a single sermon in the case of so vast a theme? The preacher requires plenty of elbow room in handling a topic of that kind. A course of sermons is the only solution. The same is true with regard to other subjects, such as the Lord's Prayer, or the Apostles' Creed, or the great doctrines of the Bible.

There are numerous biblical themes which lend themselves admirably to courses of sermons. The Psalms are excellent for this purpose. So are the parables of our Lord, including some of the lesser known ones. The same is true of the miracles; for example, the seven 'signs' of St. John's Gospel would make an interesting course. Bible characters also offer enormous scope. How about a Lent series on characters of the passion? Or a series after Easter on the resurrection appearances of our Lord? Or a series could be devoted to key texts of the Bible, or to vital questions of the Bible; or to the turning-points in our Lord's ministry; or to some notable converts in the Acts. These are no more than suggestions, intended to indicate how plentiful is the available material.

A final word must be added on a matter of special importance for the day in which we live. The Sunday services of morning and evening prayer, attended as they so often are by a fairly mixed congregation, offer in many parishes a particular opportunity for evangelism. Not all who come to such services, whether regularly or occasionally, are likely to be committed Christians. In any case, we need constantly to remind ourselves that 'a large number of Church people also require to be converted, in the sense of their possessing that personal knowledge of Christ which can be ours only by the dedication of the whole self, whatever the cost ... The aim of evangelism must be to appeal to all, within as well as without the Church, for that decision for Christ which shall make the state of salvation we call conversion the usual experience of the normal Christian.'[11]

Parochial evangelism is not a sporadic effort but a continuing process; and an important part of that process is fulfilled by the regular preaching of the Gospel throughout the course of the year, in season and out of season. There is surely something seriously lacking in our preaching ministry if the note of evangelical appeal is never or seldom heard, if there is no sort of summons to personal faith and committal. As Christ's ambassadors it is our duty and privilege to appeal to men on His behalf: '*Be reconciled to God!*' A sermon, remarks Professor Farmer, should have something of the quality of a knock on the door.[12] Now the purpose of a knock is to receive an answer; and the answer which the preacher of the Gospel has the right to expect from his hearers is the opening of the door to Christ as Saviour and Lord.

There will be occasions when the sermon is directly evangelistic in character, intended to bring people to the point of a definite commitment to Christ. A Sunday evening guest service provides a ready opening for this. The

[11] *Towards the Conversion of England* (London, 1945), p. 37.
[12] H. H. Farmer: *The Servant of the Word*, p. 65.

opportunity should not be neglected. Despite the widespread indifference to the things of God on the part of the great masses, we may be sure that there are those in our churches who are deeply aware of that 'God-shaped blank' in their souls and who are anxiously seeking something more satisfying than the world can offer them: peace of heart and mind, freedom from their fears and frustrations, a sense of purpose in life.

Is there an answer to their quest? There is—but one answer only. It is embodied in the Gospel of redeeming grace. To proclaim that Gospel is the preacher's task. To the fulfilment of that task every preacher is called. 'I charge you in the presence of God and of Christ Jesus who is to judge the living and the dead, and by His appearing and His kingdom: preach the word, be urgent in season and out of season, convince, rebuke, and exhort . . . do the work of an evangelist, fulfil your ministry' (II Tim. 4: 1, 2, 5).

CHAPTER FIVE

PREACHING TODAY

PREACHING today is, in one sense, no different from preaching in any other age. This is due to two constant factors involved in preaching.

The first is that the preacher's message—both *kerygma* and *didache*—remains unchanged from age to age. That message is the living and abiding Word of God; and in its primary sense that Word, as we have seen, is none other than Jesus Christ Himself, the same yesterday, today and for ever. The preacher who is true to his calling and stands in the apostolic tradition proclaims a Gospel which is as much good news for the twentieth century as it was for the first.

This, at any rate, is the firm conviction of the evangelical churchman. Where the message is concerned—as distinct from method—he does not feel inclined to trim his sails to catch the passing breeze. He is aware that not all share his old-fashioned viewpoint. There are those who maintain that the historic Christian faith is subject to modification and re-interpretation in the light of man's developing knowledge of the world and the revolutionary movements of modern secular society. As a result, we are now being offered new images of God, new patterns of truth, new ethical ideals.

Evangelicals are neither particularly excited nor unduly alarmed by these well-meaning attempts to rewrite

Christianity. To them, there is a *givenness* about the Gospel which is untouched by the latest theological, psychological, or sociological ideas. They feel pretty much as St. Paul did about those who preach 'another Jesus' or 'a different gospel' (II Cor. 11:4). They stand by the old faith—the faith once for all delivered. They are determined to know nothing but Jesus Christ and Him crucified.

No doubt this attitude lays them open to the accusation of being narrow in their outlook and over-dogmatic. They are prepared to face the charge. They would plead in their defence that they bear witness to eternal truth which is unchanging and unchangeable. As P. T. Forsyth wrote: 'It is into the Bible world of the eternal redemption that the preacher must bring his people. The only preaching which is up to date for every time is the preaching of this eternity, which is opened to us in the Bible alone—the eternal of holy love, grace and redemption, the eternal and immutable morality of saving grace for our indelible sin.'[1]

One further point deserves to be recognized here. The givenness of the preacher's message derives not only from the final revelation given in the historic Christ but also from the apostolic witness to the historic Christ. This apostolic witness is authoritative for the Church in a way in which none other is. The preacher is not at liberty to place his own interpretation alongside it as of equal worth. The apostolic witness is part of the divine revelation enshrined in the New Testament and is as unique and unchanging as the Christ to which it points.

The other constant factor is—*people*. People are much

[1] P. T. Forsyth: *op. cit.*, p. 33.

the same now as they have always been. Each generation, of course, considers itself to be different and unique; and in some measure this is true. Yet it is a remarkable fact that fundamentally human nature does not change. In a world of continual flux and movement, subject to all manner of political, social, and technological upheavals, people themselves remain at heart the same. Nothing is more clear in our own day than that man's intellectual advance and scientific achievement are not matched by any corresponding spiritual or moral progress. Man is still, as Jesus so plainly saw, a sinner in need of a saviour—sick in soul, spiritually blind, lost to God. The Bible's portrait of humanity in its fallen state is perpetually up to date. This is why the Bible still speaks so convincingly to man's condition today.

But that is not all. The Bible's view of man is not, ultimately, a pessimistic one. It sees in him, through the redemption that is in Christ Jesus, vast hopes and possibilities. Whatever he is by nature, there is no doubt about what he may become by grace: a member of Christ, the child of God, and an inheritor of the kingdom of heaven. It is this fact that makes the preaching of the Gospel such an amazing privilege, such a thrilling task.

THE CONTEMPORARY SITUATION

The Gospel is timeless and people are much the same in every generation. Yet it remains true, as we have hinted, that each age has its own particular characteristics, its own spiritual climate and intellectual outlook. And the Church must take account of this. It must be involved in the world *as it is*—not in the unreal world of a bygone age.

Here is a challenge to the preacher. His job, as it has

been said, is that of bringing the given Gospel to the given world. He may not be content with the world as it is, but he is compelled to recognize it and accept it as it is before he sets about the task of making it better.

What about the world of our own day? This is not the place to make a fresh assessment of the contemporary scene or analyse the modern mood from the preacher's point of view. Many attempts have been made to do that in recent works on preaching. Thus the Archbishop of York declares that ours is a frightened, lonely, disillusioned age and that man, in spite of his achievements and discoveries, is increasingly aware of his insignificance.[2] Professor Farmer, writing as far back as 1941, said much the same thing. He described men and women as being oppressed with a sense of the futility and meaninglessness of human existence, shocked and frightened by an awareness of the forces of evil and unreason at work in history, and yearning for security.[3] Yet it is also true that modern man tends to be self-sufficient and to recognize no need of God. He is his own god. His thinking is conditioned by the 'scientific' attitude and outlook, with its glorification of human knowledge and its blind faith in human reason.[4]

These are factors which the preacher must take into his reckoning as he faces his congregation. It is useless to pretend that the contemporary situation is an easy one. This is not an age of faith. The circumstances of life inculcate a secular rather than a religious outlook. The Christian Gospel is challenged by rival creeds and

[2] Donald Coggan: *Stewards of Grace*, pp. 15-17.
[3] H. H. Farmer: *op. cit.*, p. 131.
[4] See Norman Pittenger: *op. cit.*, p. 46f.

ideologies. For modern man, religion smacks of superstition. He is content to interpret life in humanistic and materialistic terms. As far as he is concerned, the things unseen and eternal are utterly unreal.

Such a situation may well compel the preacher to do some hard thinking and to reconsider how best to present his God-given message in a way that will render it relevant, contemporary, intelligible. He should make it his business to keep abreast of current thought and to study man's world as well as God's Word, in order to be able to communicate the one to the other. Many a parson is so hopelessly out of touch with the everyday world of his congregation that he is incapable of entering into their problems and of meeting their needs. He would do well to widen his reading of books, newspapers and magazines and to mix freely with all kinds of people—as our Lord did with those of His day—in order to learn more about their thought-forms and their way of life.

This is part of what the modern situation requires of the preacher. What it does *not* require of him is to abandon the Word of God for the word of man, or to water down the Gospel, or to produce some new tailor-made religion designed to fit the scientific mind. That way lies disaster and failure. The faith that overcomes the world and wins the hearts of men is not (to use some words of Professor James Stewart) a 'pallid, anaemic Christianity' consisting of 'religious generalities and innocuous platitudes', but the faith of the cross and the empty tomb and the pentecostal fullness. That faith, old yet ever new, the preacher must proclaim still with urgency and authority.

How can he do so? By his constant realization of his commission as an ambassador of Christ. An ambassador is essentially a man under authority. His mission is not of his choosing: he is sent. The message he delivers does not originate with him: it is given him. That being so, the quality required of him above all others is *loyalty*—loyalty to the sovereign or government whose envoy he is and loyalty in the discharge of the task, the delivery of the message, entrusted to him.

What a magnificent ideal this represents for the Christian preacher! No wonder he can speak not in halting or apologetic tones but with the note of authority. 'This certainty of calling,' wrote Martin Luther, 'may be the possession of every minister of God's Word if he deliver the message as he receives it, even as a King's ambassador. For such an ambassador speaks not of himself, or as a private person, but for his King, and in his King's name. As representing the King he is honoured and set in a place he would not occupy as a private person. Wherefore, let the preacher of the Gospel be certain that his calling is from God.'[5]

THE PREACHER AS A MAN OF GOD

Preaching is not, as we have emphasized, simply a human activity. Yet when all is said and done, much does depend upon the preacher: not so much upon his ability or personality as upon his spiritual qualities, upon what he *is* as a man of God. To revert to the analogy we have been pursuing: an ambassador cannot fulfil his duties faithfully unless he is in close and continuous contact with those who sent him. Nor can the Christian preacher make full proof of his ministry unless he himself is in touch with

[5] Martin Luther: *Commentary on the Epistle to the Galatians*, edited by J. P. Fallowes, p. 2.

the throne of God and comes before his congregation, in Karl Barth's phrase, 'as a man who has been pierced by the Word of God'.

This implies that the preacher is a man of prayer who knows what it is to spend time in the secret place. It is said of Dr. Alexander Whyte of Edinburgh that on one occasion his sermon created such a profound impression that after the service someone remarked to him, 'Dr. Whyte, you preached today as if you had come straight from the presence of God!' Shyly and quietly the preacher answered, 'Perhaps I had.'

Spiritual power is the ultimate secret. No preacher can be content with his ministry so long as it is 'in word only' —even though that word may be perfectly true and most eloquently expressed. It must be his earnest desire that the Word of God should come to men through him 'not in word only, but also in power and in the Holy Ghost, and in much assurance' (I Thess. 1:5). Clearly something more is needed in the preaching of the Word than correct techniques, or biblical orthodoxy, or human learning. That something more is spiritual unction—having the love of God shed abroad in our hearts through the Holy Spirit whom He has given us. Without that divine anointing and energizing preaching is but verbosity. There is hardly need to elaborate the point. Let the following quotations from the Scriptures serve to enforce it:

'The Spirit of the Lord is upon me, because He has anointed me to preach good news . . .' (Lk. 4:18, quoting Is. 61:1).

'You shall receive power when the Holy Spirit has come upon you; and you shall be my witnesses . . .' (Acts 1:8).

'My speech and my message were not in plausible words

of wisdom, but in demonstration of the Spirit and power' (I Cor. 2:4).

'... those who preached the good news to you through the Holy Spirit sent from heaven' (I Pet. 1:12).

Here is seen the peculiar function of the Holy Spirit in relation to the ministry of the Word: to empower the preacher, to accompany the words spoken, and to apply the message to the hearts of the hearers. Well does Professor Von Allmen lay down this further thesis: *Without the work of the Holy Spirit the Word which God has spoken to the world in His Son cannot be effectively translated or made present.* 'In preaching, that is to say in translating and making present the Word of God,' he comments, 'we are not only ministers of Christ but also agents of the Holy Spirit and His work ... This requires from us, before, during, and after the sermon, intense supplication: there is no true preaching without *epiklesis*. But this fact is also reassuring: in carrying out our arduous work as preachers we are not alone.'[6]

A WORD TO THE CLERGY

I conclude this chapter with some words addressed respectively to the preacher and the congregation, the man in the pulpit and the people in the pews. In the ministry of the Word, as we have already noted, a particular responsibility belongs to both.

As far as the preacher is concerned, here are six simple, practical counsels summing up and reinforcing much of what has already been said in this little book.

Be biblical. Preach the Word! Stress has been laid repeatedly upon this in these pages. Yet if there is one

[6] J.-J. Von Allmen: *op. cit.*, p. 31.

point above all others which I wish to insist upon it is that the preacher stands under the authority of the Word of God, that he is to regard himself as the humble servant of the Word, and that preaching is nothing unless it be a genuine ministry of the Word.

It is not enough to talk about the Bible. The Bible itself must be taught, expounded, interpreted, applied. In recent years a good deal of lip-service has been paid to 'biblical preaching' and there is general agreement that this is what is needed today; but I am by no means certain that this is what is being done in the majority of churches. Let the following words from the Ordinal recall us clergy to the study and preaching of the Bible with renewed devotion:

'And seeing that you cannot by any other means compass the doing of so weighty a work, pertaining to the salvation of man, but with doctrine and exhortation taken out of the holy Scriptures, and with a life agreeable to the same; consider how studious ye ought to be in reading and learning the Scriptures . . . that, by daily reading and weighing of the Scriptures, ye may wax riper and stronger in your ministry'.[1]

Be earnest. Give of your best to the ministry of the Word. Magnify your office as Christ's ambassador. It is reasonably certain that if the clergyman does not take his preaching seriously, his hearers are not likely to do so either. They know well enough whether his heart is in the business: whether he goes into the pulpit because he has something to say, or simply because he has to say something. They are very ready to recognize a lack of zest for the job, or—worse still—a lack of sincerity.

[1] From the Bishop's Charge in the Ordering of Priests.

On the other hand, when the heart of the preacher is 'strangely warmed' with the love of God, the congregation will know it, and will also begin to catch fire. There is a lot of truth in the old adage, 'like priest, like people'. Was that luke-warm church at Laodicea due in some measure to its having a luke-warm preacher to its minister? Richard Baxter, the great Puritan preacher, pleaded with his brother ministers: 'I earnestly beseech you all, in the name of God, and for the sake of your people's souls, that you will not slightly slubber over this work, but do it vigorously and with all your might, and make it your great and serious business.'[8] And Baxter himself set a noble example as exemplified in his passionate resolve.

> I preach as if I ne'er should preach again,
> And as a dying man to dying men.

Be simple. Preach in an intelligible manner, in language which the congregation will understand. Remember that it was said of our Lord, 'the common people heard Him gladly'. Was not that a tribute to the fact that He spoke to them in a way they could understand? The same characteristic marked the apostolic preaching, and also the apostolic writings. It is an impressive fact that the language of the New Testament as a whole is not the classical Greek but the common speech of the day, the language of the home and the market.

It has been suggested that the preacher should be a master of two languages: the language of divine revelation preserved in Holy Scripture, and the language of the world spoken by the man in the street. His aim is not to

[8] Quoted by J. S. Stewart: *Heralds of God*, pp. 112–13.

dazzle his hearers with a display of high-sounding verbosity or confuse them by using a mass of theological jargon. His task is to clarify, not to mystify.

It is only too possible in this so-called intellectual age for the parson to imagine that he must be a bit high-brow and adopt a semi-academic style if he is to appeal to his hearers. This is a fallacy. By all means let him treat them as intelligent people and not preach down to them; but at the same time let him not mistake worldly learning for spiritual understanding. The average man in the pew, for all his education, is painfully ignorant of the Bible and the things of God. The preacher must exercise self-discipline here and resist the temptation to display his learning, real or imaginary. James Denney's piercing words are worth recalling: 'No man can bear witness to himself and Jesus Christ at one and the same time. No man, at one and the same time, can convey the impression that he himself is clever and that Christ is mighty to save.'

Be interesting. Remember that you have to put up a fight to win the attention of your people. There is apparently a strange psychological mechanism by which many in the congregation automatically 'switch off' when the sermon begins, and lose all sense of concentration. It may be that many of them are tired. Probably their spiritual appetite is blunted. And this means that the preacher must strenuously set to work to be interesting, so as to awaken and hold their attention.

Dullness is one of the worst sins of the pulpit. If the preacher fails to grip his people at the outset he might as well give up. In any case he has no right to complain that they are not interested if he himself is drowsy and prosy. In an age when people are no longer in the habit of attending church as a matter of course, he can hardly expect them to come simply to be bored by dry-as-dust sermons.

Yet why should preaching be dull? The message with which the preacher is entrusted is not dull. The New Testament actually calls it 'good news'; and good news is far from being dull. It is exciting, stimulating, tremendous! And what God in Christ has done for man's salvation—and is still waiting to do—is the most amazing good news of all. Once let the preacher be gripped by the sheer wonder of it all and he will not fail to arrest and hold the interest of those who hear him. In his description of the preaching of John Donne in old St. Paul's Cathedral Isaac Walton said that he spoke in such a way 'as showed his own heart was possessed with those very thoughts and joys that he laboured to distil into others'. No one accused the learned Dean of being dull!

Be positive. The pulpit is not the place for denunciation and debate. Its supreme function is the declaration of what St. Paul called 'the word of truth, the gospel of (our) salvation'. Truth: gospel (good news): salvation—those are strongly positive concepts, and they are the very heart of the Christian proclamation.

There is a type of preaching which is largely controversial and censorious, which delights in fault-finding, hair-splitting, heresy-hunting, and which is never happy unless it is attacking something or somebody. Admittedly error must be refuted, and controversy cannot always be shunned. But the best way to overthrow falsehood is by preaching the truth, and the positive approach is always more effective in the end than the negative. Moreover, when some controversial issue is at stake, let the preacher first be sure that the question is big enough and important enough to merit his attention, and then see that he handles it understandingly, in a constructive manner, and with a heart full of love.

Negative preaching will never win souls, or edify the Church, or advance the honour of the Lord. The Gospel itself is positive. It tells of what God *is*, of what He has *done*, of what He *gives*. Preach it positively. Preach the grace of God. Preach the redemption that is in Christ Jesus. Preach the forgiveness of sins and the new birth. Preach the dynamic of the Spirit-filled life. Preach the heavenly kingdom both as a present reality and as a future hope. These are the strong positive notes which sounded in the apostolic proclamation and which should find an echo in your own. Always have a definite, constructive aim in view, and let that aim be as clear to your hearers as it is to yourself.

Be practical. Apply the truth as you proclaim it. Show the relevance of the ancient Scriptures to our own times and to the lives of those to whom you speak. Preaching must never become remote from reality. It is concerned with the here and now as well as with the eternal realm: with the affairs of men as well as with the things of God. The preacher's aim is not simply to explain a passage of Scripture but to meet a human need. It is certainly part of his business to show what the Christian Gospel has to say about such practical matters as money, work, marriage, divorce, family life, the state, war, race, gambling, drink, and so on.

We have stressed the importance of study; but it is possible for the parson to get so wrapped up in his studies, so absorbed in biblical and theological questions, that he loses sight of people and the world outside. It is also possible for him to take refuge in evangelism to the extent that his preaching virtually lacks all teaching content, or ethical demands. Sometimes the preaching of simple 'gospel sermons' is in fact a form of escapism, or a mark of sheer laziness. It is true, people need to be converted. But they also need to be instructed and edified and equipped for the battle of life.

John Wesley wrote: '*We* know no gospel without salvation from sin.' For him, salvation involved holiness, and Christianity was a social religion. 'The gospel knows no religion but social, no holiness but social holiness,' he said. Evangelical preaching must never lack this down-to-earth quality, this ethical note, this passion for personal holiness and social righteousness. If it is true *biblical* preaching it assuredly will not do so. Far from being remote from the world it will be closely related to the world; for the Son of God for our salvation identified Himself with our flesh and made clear once and for all that religion and life can never be separated.

A WORD TO THE LAITY

Preaching requires an audience. It is far from being a one-way traffic. It does not all depend upon the preacher. He indeed is the divine instrument, the medium of communication through whom the Word of God is spoken. But the Word is not spoken in a vacuum. It is spoken to people—and they have their own particular responsibility to fulfil in the ministry of the Word.

Again, as we have insisted, preaching is part of the total activity of worship. It is designed for the glory of God—not for the glory of man. Its object is to lift up the hearts of the hearers to God in penitence, hope and adoration. That is why P. T. Forsyth could describe preaching as 'the organised Hallelujah of an ordered community' and as 'the Church confessing its faith'.

What precisely is the role of the congregation?

Its first duty is to *listen* to the preaching in a receptive and responsive manner. Nothing so kills a sermon or disheartens a preacher as an apathetic congregation. 'He that hath ears to hear, let him hear.' The familiar words of our Lord are relevant whenever the Word of God is preached. They imply a certain attitude on the part of the hearer. They recognize that it is possible to listen outwardly without hearing inwardly, that is, without responding to what is said. When, however, preaching does win that response, something happens—and not only to the hearer. By his response he gives back something to the preacher. And the preacher knows it.

'Any preacher of experience will bear witness to this fact,' writes the Archbishop of York, 'that in Church A one Sunday, having prepared himself and his sermon with care and prayer, he finds that his words rebound like a fives ball from the wall of the court. In Church B the following Sunday, the preparation of himself and of his sermon having been the same as during the previous week, he finds a receptivity to the Word of God and a response to it so manifest and real as to be almost tangible. What is the reason for this? No doubt many factors are involved. I suspect, however, that one of the most important is this—the members of congregation A have never grasped the fact that preaching is a function, a corporate activity of the Church . . . But at Church B the members of the congregation know that prayerful dedication on the part of the preacher is not enough—something is demanded of *them*. Preaching is a *corporate* activity.'[9]

The congregation has another responsibility: to *pray* for the preacher and for the ministry of the Word. When C. H. Spurgeon was asked on one occasion how he could account for the manifest blessing attending his preaching ministry at the Metropolitan Tabernacle, he answered very simply, 'My people pray for me.' There were no doubt other elements in the situation besides prayer; but equally certainly prayer was a factor which could not be discountenanced.

Perhaps the parson in the parish has no greater comfort than to know that he is not alone in his work but that he is surrounded and upheld by a band of faithful praying people who, in a true sense, are workers together with him in the ministry of the Word. He can count upon their prayers both in the preparation of his sermons and in his actual delivery of the message. And he comes to realize increasingly that such prayer fellowship not only gives him spiritual freedom and power in the pulpit but also creates the kind of atmosphere in which the Holy Spirit can do His work.

There are other ways in which the laity can be of help. One of these is by *encouraging* the parson in his preaching ministry—and often he needs such encouragement. They can do this by showing a lively interest in the sermons they hear and by being ready to talk over points of special interest; perhaps by suggesting suitable topics from time to time; certainly by an occasional word of thanks for help received. Should it not also be the aim of the laity to bring others to church to hear the Word of God? And ought

[9] Donald Coggan: *Stewards of Grace*, pp. 87–8.

there not to be more regular opportunities for sermon discussion, so that preaching can be in very deed a two-way traffic, a genuine dialogue between pastor and people?

In this book we have urged the clergy to take the preaching office seriously. The same plea must be made in the case of the laity. It must not be overlooked that there is a responsibility attaching to the hearing as well as to the proclamation of the Gospel. There might well be better preachers in our churches if there were better listeners.

Our prayer to God must constantly be: 'Make, we beseech Thee, all Bishops and Pastors diligently to preach Thy holy Word, and the people obediently to follow the same, that they may receive the crown of everlasting glory; through Jesus Christ our Lord.'[10]

[10] From the Collect of St. Peter's Day.

CHRISTIAN FOUNDATIONS

The first titles in this series are:

1. **CONFESS YOUR SINS**
   The Way of Reconciliation
   By John R. W. Stott

2. **BUT FOR THE GRACE OF GOD...**
   Divine Initiative and Human Need
   By Philip Edgcumbe Hughes

3. **THE BODY OF CHRIST**
   A New Testament Image of the Church
   By Alan Cole

4. **CALLED TO SERVE**
   Ministry and Ministers in the Church
   By Michael Green

5. **AFTER DEATH**
   A Sure and Certain Hope?
   By J. A. Motyer

6. **GOD HAS SPOKEN**
   Revelation and the Bible
   By J. I. Packer

7. **GOD AND MAMMON**
   The Christian Mastery of Money
   By K. F. W. Prior

8. **CHRIST'S AMBASSADORS**
   The Priority of Preaching
   By Frank Colquhoun

9. **SEX AND SANITY**
   The Christian View of Sexual Morality
   By Stuart Barton Babbage